How to Think

How to Think

Building Your Mental Muscle

Stephen Reid

An imprint of **Pearson Education**

London · New York · San Francisco · Toronto · Sydney
Tokyo · Singapore · Hong Kong · Cape Town · Madrid
Paris · Milan · Munich · Amsterdam

PEARSON EDUCATION LIMITED

Head Office:	*London Office:*
Edinburgh Gate	128 Long Acre
Harlow CM20 2JE	London WC2E 9AN
Tel: +44 (0)1279 623623	Tel: +44 (0)20 7447 2000
Fax: +44 (0)1279 431059	Fax: +44 (0)20 7240 5771

Website: www.business-minds.com

First published in Great Britain in 2002

The right of Stephen Reid to be identified as author of this work has been asserted by him in accordance with the Copyright, Designs and Patents Act 1988.

ISBN: 0 273 65484 5

British Library Cataloguing in Publication Data
A CIP catalogue record for this book can be obtained from the British Library.

10 9 8 7 6 5 4 3 2

Designed by designdeluxe, Bath
Typeset by Pantek Arts Ltd, Maidstone, Kent, England
Printed and bound in Great Britain by Bell & Bain Ltd, Glasgow

The Publishers' policy is to use paper manufactured from sustainable forests.

Dedicated to my mentor Martin Scott at Ashridge

About the author

Stephen Reid works with both public and private sector organisations on thinking skills projects to improve the development of leadership, innovation, management creativity and strategy in the UK, Europe, the USA and the Middle East. He is an experienced business manager and has run successful operations with Eli Lilly, Johnson and Johnson and Fisons. Stephen has postgraduate teaching interests with Nottingham Business School the UK Strategic Planning Society and occasionally works with Ashridge Management College. He is a popular speaker at conferences on Innovation and has published articles and book reviews in *Strategy*.

Contents

Acknowledgements

This book is about tools and techniques that we can adopt in our thinking. In considering how we think, it is worth reflecting on the wealth of external experiences that are available to us all.

We experience our highest levels of thinking when inspired. Inspiration offers itself up to us from many sources and in many ways. In my particular case one of my bigger sources of inspiration is other people. I am especially indebted to Martin Scott of Ashridge who has been my inspiration and mentor since I began this particular journey. Meeting Martin Scott in 1991 was the catalyst that helped me begin to see that if it was possible to pass on creative ability, it must also be possible to teach and transfer other thinking skills.

One of the hardest lessons of all, which I have discovered a little too late in life, is that of humility. For this I'm indebted to a former lover who kept saying when I was perched upon my highest horse, 'Lord, it's hard to be humble'. She is right.

I would also like to thank all my family, friends and neighbours who patiently helped me screen the chapters during the book's evolutionary period. Special thanks go to Rachael Stock, Chris French, Julie Smith, Antony Healy, Rachel Russell, Malcolm Hornby and Sally Mackinley. Thanks also to Steve Carter, Marie Shelton, Graham Rawlinson and Barry Johnson for their contributions. Also to Ralph Bedrock at Nottingham Business School for his suggestions on orienteering and for his patient indulgence over the years.

Introduction

Welcome to my world *How to Think* is aimed at anyone who wants to be successful at work and 'have a life' at the same time. *How to Think* is a guide about basic thinking patterns you can employ along with a tool kit of mental models that will help you begin to understand a variety of everyday situations. I hope that some of the ideas in my book will help or encourage you on your own personal journey.

Everyday situations in which you may wish to improve your ability to think could include:

- strategy development
- decision making
- problem solving
- negotiation
- relationships
- managing the balance between work and real life
- dealing with incomplete information
- generating creativity.

In addition, you may want to feel better equipped to handle the following:

- ambiguity
- uncertainty, certainty and risk
- truth and relative truth
- error.

How to Think is a guide that contains tools and techniques that you can use right away to deal with a variety of life's wrinkles. Use this book to help you deal with life when everything is changing; to answer questions such as 'How do I deal with uncertainty and ambiguity?' or 'Where am I going with my relationships?' These and many more questions are addressed in the following chapters. If you are a browser, each chapter can be read in isolation. However I would recommend you read Chapters 2 and 3 early on.

We get a manual with a car, a hi-fi, a cooker and a mobile phone. I've even had a manual for a cooking pan! A lot of intelligent people clearly thought it was important for us consumers to have a manual for pans and CD players and spent heaps of money producing them. So when it comes to the most important aspect of our lives, namely how we use our minds, why isn't there an easy-to-read manual? Whatever the explanation, this book aims to begin to fill that particular real and pressing need.

Have you ever heard an older person declare 'If only I'd known then what I know now I would be much better off'? Well, this book is designed with this in mind. No one ever taught me how to think and probably, like the majority of people, I just got on with it. Having stumbled and tripped, I gave a lot of thought to how and where I could have done things differently, including the way I thought.

How to Think is a book for any normal healthy person who wants to improve her or his lot in life. It provides a variety of templates and patterns with which you can develop your own answers to life's complexities. While I am not a professional psychologist, I have made a second career out of untangling knotty business problems and over the last six years have run numerous thinking skills workshops at senior management level in the UK, Europe and the USA. All of the methods and concepts are based on pragmatic experience and are tried and tested in business or in business workshops.

As you turn the pages you will see a lot of illustrations. There are several reasons for this. First and foremost, I believe pictures are more powerful than mere words. In addition, by employing imagery as well as words, we can improve the way we think and the quality and scope of our thoughts. Once we learn to enrich our thoughts, we can also enhance the way we communicate with others. Language is a relatively recent social evolutionary trait that has come very much to the fore in the way we use our minds. However, the way we process images pre-dates language because, as a physically inferior species, our survival in our very recent past would have depended a great deal upon visual accuracy and prediction. I suggest that by learning how to employ

Pictures are more powerful than mere words

a combination of concepts, ideas and imagery alongside our relatively recent language skills we are able to improve the way we think. Even if you adopt only one of the models an improvement can be made.

Opening a book lets you some of the way into the mind of its author. So 'Welcome to my world, come on in!', turn the pages and let me show you around. For example, I am not too shy to reveal that I have made *lots* of mistakes in my life. I have thought about these, learned, moved on and made plenty more. Despite the hard nature of some of these experiences, I believe I am all the better for the lessons I have learned and for the blessings delivered by faith, hard work and persistence. I wish, though, that I had read *How to Think* when I was much younger. No doubt I would still have made just as many mistakes, but I suspect my lessons would have been of a different kind and at a much higher level!

I dwell on the subject of 'mistakes' because error can cause us to produce unnecessary barriers within our perception. If you do nothing in this life, there is little risk of making a mistake. As a counter-balance to my making so many mistakes, I find I am frequently amused at my own shortcomings and hopefully all the more aware of what is going on and open to what is available around me.

How to Think connects patterns of thinking with your choice of behaviour and personal orientation. One of the skills that will emerge as you use the techniques in this book is a heightened sense of self-awareness.

If you want to develop your mind, being open to new ideas is important, no matter what your age. Being open to inspiration is another skill that you can reacquire or enhance by improving your self-awareness and your thinking.

To inspire and be inspired and to remain open, in case you forgot, were skills you used all the time in childhood; these skills are still in you now. I hope that in your journey you will improve or rediscover these and other skills. Also I trust you will see many of the ideas in my book as common sense, once you think about them.

Welcome to my world.

Stephen Reid
October 2001

Invitation

How to Think contains tools, tips and suggestions.

No one person can claim to have all the answers to such a vast topic as 'How to Think' so I would therefore welcome your suggestions.

Please e-mail me via my website: http://www.spreid.com

Uncork the genie – don't hit the buffers

We believe we are a thinking species, but for much of the time our minds are running on automatic. Only rarely do we access our full potential for original thinking. The human tendency is to consciously think only by exception. Most of the time we employ a relatively effortless automated reaction system for dealing with the mundane aspects of everyday life.

This is significant because life is demanding more and more from us. Working harder is no longer a valid solution to increased pressure, especially if you are already putting in all the hours you can. The solution is to work smarter, not harder.

So when was the last time you asked yourself 'How do I think?' Most of us tend to stick to one familiar pattern that uses only part of our potential. This book is about how to effectively use more of your mind.

My observation of high-performance people is that they seem to be able to work smarter and to draw upon a variety of intellectual resources. Their ability is not just a question of possessing one major ability such as IQ. Often there is a mixture of different skills that together add up to their being 'smart about life'. One major observation, and the central thesis of this book, is that often their thinking will exist within patterns or models that consistently work for them. When faced with a new problem, smart professionals will quickly seek out the appropriate model or an architecture within which to deploy their thoughts. As you read through this book you will see a wide range of patterns, shapes and models to help you improve the way you think.

As a professional, you will be in a more powerful position if you are able to generate choices and subsequently make good decisions. With more choices a decision can be based on a variety of options instead of being just a pre-programmed knee-jerk response. When we have the opportunity to think we also have the scope to choose our subsequent behaviour. We can begin to shape our world.

In order to be more in control of a situation at work or within our personal lives, we first need to understand and be in control of ourselves. This is an essential step in the transition towards working smarter. People who create choices for themselves and for the behaviour they display can be described as smart.

So why is it that we tend to react without thinking? Some of the reasons lie in our most basic biology. Our most fundamental instinct of self-preservation is wired to react to danger even before higher-level conscious thought engages. Primitive brain systems remain active despite the presence of higher thinking (cortical) functions. The primitive lower levels of our brain can actually hi-jack and override our ability to think when faced with perceived extreme 'danger'. There is a perfectly good reason for this pattern of behaviour – when faced with real danger we survive first and rationalize second. Our ancestors who did this the other way around ended up as lunch and were not able to pass on their genes!

Another reason for not engaging our full thinking potential is that our minds are arranged to conserve energy and we do this by developing efficient patterns of thought and behaviour. For example, having learned how to drive, we automate the actions required to the point that we need not engage conscious thinking about what we are actually doing on routine journeys. Only if something exceptional happens, such as the sudden potential for an accident, do we engage full conscious thinking again.

Our minds are alert to unusual events or objects because they might conceivably harm or benefit us. Novelties create tension and uncertainty. Consequently we are driven to expend the necessary energy to overcome this uncertainty until we 'know' the new event, and can slot it safely into a known pattern or context or dismiss it as unimportant.

Accumulated automated ideas and patterns of behaviour constitute our experience. People are hired based on how much (automated) experience they possess. Organizations place a high value on the ability to perform tasks fast and effortlessly, almost without thinking. Our automated experiences are valuable, but automated thinking and predetermined behavioural routines can cause major problems too.

As a species we do think, but often only by exception

We have chosen to label ourselves Homo Sapiens (thinking man), which is partly true. As a species we do think, but often only by exception.

Active thinking demands we hold a state of 'uncertainty' open long enough to study something new. Uncertainty and openness leave us feeling vulnerable, which can create a sense of tension, causing us to lose energy. This sort of tension can be exciting or frightening. When we confront novelty we increase uncertainty, which puts our minds and our bodies on full alert. This is expensive as we spend lots of our mental energy. Fully engaged thinking is actually very demanding, hard work – you *will* feel drained when you have a lot to think about. Our minds have found a way of saving time and energy by automating our perception and behaviour using familiar collections of patterns. These familiar patterns help us, but they also have the potential to hinder us.

Existing knowledge can block new learning

Since many people fail to think about thinking, we are left unaware of our additional abilities and how we might fully engage them. There is a very simple but powerful concept barrier to be crossed for many people at this stage. When we are unaware of something, we do not know what are the right questions to ask, let alone what the answers might be. The simple barrier we need to cross is our failure to realize there may be pre-programmed patterns operating at the forefront of our thinking and that these need to be disengaged before we can engage in original thinking.

To illustrate how not knowing can limit us, look at the drawing below and follow the instructions. Please draw in the fish's eyes. (Yes, it's OK to draw on the book if you bought it!) Draw roughly where the other fins would go. Now draw in the mouth. When you have completed these two steps, follow the next instruction underneath the picture.

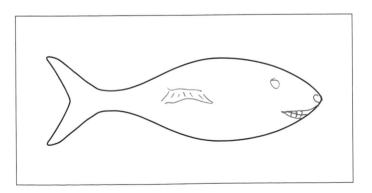

If you think the next instruction is funny, that's OK, because many people laugh at it! Sound travels better underwater than in the air: draw in the fish's ears. Fish really do have a hearing system. So draw in where you think the fish picks up sound.

The trouble is our current knowledge has not prepared most of us to answer this particular question. Even if we started to research this question, most of us would probably begin to look in the wrong place for the wrong thing. Fish do not have earflaps protruding out of the side of their heads, but they do have an efficient hearing system arranged as a line of sensory cells, called the 'lateral line', that runs horizontally down the mid-line on both sides of its body. So next time you eat a fish, look for the line of darker-brown colouring that separates the two muscle masses that lie above and below this lateral line. Within this lateral line are the hearing cells.

> **Tip** When faced with a new learning opportunity, ask yourself whether it is simply an extension of earlier knowledge or could the situation be something completely new to you? Your existing knowledge will help in the first and probably hinder in the second case. If the situation is novel, try to experience it as if you were quite young. Suspending judgement is easier to say than do, but is worthwhile. The most useful answer is actually to admit 'Honestly, I don't know'.

The fish example illustrates that what we do know can interfere with what we *do not* know. This simple game also demonstrates that knowledge can easily be transferred. When faced with questions such as this, the smart approach is:

- Accept we do not know the answer.
- Tell others you don't know.
- Do not rely upon your ability to guess based on prior knowledge.

As a species, we continue to prosper because we share what we know and what we do not know.

Shared knowledge
Knowledge becomes something useful, something tangible, only when we share it. Otherwise it simply exists as the sum

of the ideas and experience of one individual. **Even a genius draws** Knowledge is about information sharing. New know- **on the prior work of** ledge comes from original discovery or synthesis and this **other people** requires us to use our minds actively.

Individual knowledge has a great deal to do with collective intelligence and the extent to which an individual is connected into different intelligent networks of people. A team of minds working collectively can accelerate the rate of synthesis and origination of new knowledge beyond the ability of most individual minds. Even a genius draws on the prior work of other people. Working smarter involves drawing on the knowledge of others. For the majority of people the quality of their network is key to their success.

> **Tip** The quality of your thinking will be seriously impacted by the company you keep. With this in mind, consider who you spend most of your time with and who you most rely upon at work. Has your network gone stale? Is your network or the team made up of quite similar people with similar backgrounds? If so, stir up the pot and go looking instead for people who can offer skills or experiences you lack. Are you appreciating the full scope of your network? Be patient with the diversity of people in it. Try to see the good sides within people you may have so far regarded as unusual. Learn how you can work synergistically.

The scissors graph

The case for improving the way you think and behave might come more sharply into focus if you consider your personal future. You will no doubt find work tends to become *more*, not less, demanding as time progresses. As intelligent beings, we have lots of options and choices in our lives, but we can only exercise them when we make these choices explicit. To illustrate the need for quality thinking, let us consider every manager's favourite problem – time and deadlines. Most of us consider pressure as a short-term deadline issue. However, let's map what your longer-term pressures might look like in general terms. Try the following exercise. I call it a scissors graph. This rough and ready graphing technique can be quickly and crudely applied in many different situations, but here we will look at the rest of your working life.

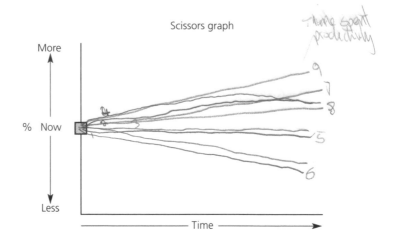

Scissors graph

The answer to each of the questions below is a trend over time, either up or down. On the graph roughly draw a series of lines or curves to represent each of these trends. Your lines or curves should start at the small square box and move from left to right. An accumulation of trends represented by lines or curves should all be displayed on the same chart, one overlaid upon the other.

The questions considered over time are:

- Over time, will work tend to get harder or easier?
- What will my workload look like?
- What time will be available to do things?
- What money will be available to do things?
- What number of people will be available to do things?
- Generally speaking, what will happen to stress levels?
- How much will be expected of me personally?
- What will happen to competition in our industry or system?

Then think of two or three other influences on your work and draw the trend for them too.

Then next to the square box on the graph above write the number of hours you personally put in at work each week. Underneath it write the number of contracted hours. Divide the two and express as a percentage.

Hours worked/week = 40 Divided by contracted hours/week = 35
= _____ %

This will describe your current load. For example, if you are putting in 50 hours a week and the contract says you get paid for 40, you are working at 125 per cent (ten hours for free!).

Every business has managers, and a major role they serve is to keep things 'on track' and to deal with a crisis. In order to deal effectively with a crisis, a manager ideally should be fresh and alert; after all, when faced with danger we would expect optimum performance – wouldn't we? So, how much more spare capacity do you have? For example, should a crisis arise, how much time is 'spare' to cope with it while maintaining the other responsibilities in your life?

Next write down how much harder you could work: 20 %

Using this information, draw a boundary on your own chart.

A typical scissors graph

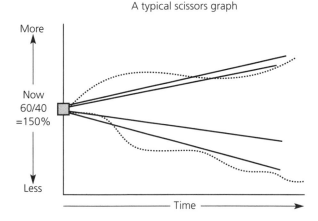

Given the trends you see in front of you, when are you going to reach a point where you will need to routinely trade off time at work with the time available in the rest of your daily living time? At which point, given the shape of the trends, might you reasonably expect to start to be ill as a consequence of the various forces and influences upon you? How would you know when you were on the wrong track? If you are currently at 60 or 70 per cent capacity, or to put it another way, you are contracted to work five eight-hour days, but you only put in three or four days, you have some time to go before the scissors graph gets you! So far I have not met anyone in this position or anyone who will admit to having 30 to 40 per cent free capacity. Most of the people I meet are currently operating at more than 120 per cent. If you have followed the

The hardest task-master in your life is likely to be yourself

exercise above, you will see quite starkly that there is a real limit to the formula of *you working harder + longer hours = increased effectiveness*. Pressure can improve performance in the short term, but while some people thrive on the adrenaline, there is ultimately a price to pay in the long term. Reliance on adrenaline is a sort of self-induced substance abuse.

Applying 'experience' and working harder to resolve difficulties will often buy time, but only a little. Relentless pressure for improvement, as illustrated by your own scissors graph, will eventually demand too much of you. In very crude terms, this sort of rough and ready graph might predict approximately when you will have your own personally induced heart attack, burnout or similar high-level crisis. The crazy thing is that the hardest taskmaster in your life is likely to be yourself. The trick is to realize what is happening and to change the rules of your own game before the work pattern gets out of hand. A fundamental component of this book is that learning how to think involves taking responsibility for your own thoughts and your own behaviours.

The only solution to the scissors trap is working smarter, *not* harder, because it is likely you are working hard enough already. Being able to harness more of our intellectual ability is therefore absolutely essential to our future well-being and happiness.

In the future, as work becomes relentlessly more competitive, time will be increasingly precious both at home and in the office. In addition, even more will be expected from us in many of our personal relationships outside of work. At work we will be expected to be managers, counsellors, mentors, coaches and leaders. At home, as well as being influenced by our parents, we will be exposed to widely publicized behavioural roles from increasing numbers of media channels. We will be expected to be caring, supportive parents who are attentive to our lovers' needs in their careers and personal life. Standing still in self-development terms is no longer an option. The tools in the rest of the book may help you on your journey.

Tip People in the range 37–55 can become vulnerable to life's not-so-subtle hints to slow down a little, such as burnout and heart attack. Watch out for the early signs. Make sure your significant other agrees with the balance of activity within your life – ask them. The in-tray will still be there long after you are not. If you both agree you need to change, plan how and then do it.

Self-awareness and separation

Performance improvement within companies can often really mean, 'How do I cope with more?' I do not believe this book would have been published had our business lives been a lot less pressured. So a guide to thinking skills written for the 21st century should provide some tips on maintaining the quality of your thinking in the face of mounting pressure.

In a lot of the work I do with management teams, I try to assess what is happening with the way people are thinking. My colleagues and I look for sub-components within the thinking and behaviour systems that have a major influence on the whole pattern. Usually there are several forces at work at any one time, bundled up under simple headings. Our skill seems to be in unbundling these influences, making

You can become the monitor of your own thoughts

them explicit and then devising thinking tools to deal with them. Because we all have within us such a perplexing mixture of interests, our thinking can sometimes feel chaotic and life can occasionally begin to look deceptively complicated. Mapping what these influences are allows us to think more clearly about our choices.

To understand the way we think I have tried to deconstruct the tangled web we unwittingly weave. In doing this, I stumbled upon an odd practice that many people may take for granted, the idea that you can become the monitor of your own thoughts. In other words, you make a serious effort to be fully aware of your own thinking – as you are thinking. I call this process 'separation'.

Actually we use separation intermittently. If I were to give you an interesting yet strange problem, your subconscious mind would work in the background to make sense of the information and would try to come up with a useful result or insight. Intuition is when you find the answer without being aware of the dialogue you have been having within yourself. Separation, while similar to intuition, differs in that you will be aware of your own conversation with yourself about your own thinking while you are actively thinking. Separation is the process where self-observation runs in parallel with thinking.

The idea of separation may sound a little absurd at first but consider those occasions when, after something went dreadfully wrong, you have remembered a little voice in the corner of your mind that had said, 'No! Don't do it!' but you chose to ignore it, much to your regret. Well, that little voice was your intuition crying out to be heard. Separation is about bringing that voice into consciousness. If you are serious about improving the quality of your thinking, then give that little voice some credibility. Actively use the idea of separation to begin to observe your own thinking.

The more you engage the conversation with your self-monitor, the more practised you will become in employing those deeper thinking resources that normally operate in the background.

Awareness enables choices, which in turn can help you live a smarter life.

Tip In order to improve the quality and scope of your thinking, try to learn to trust your intuition by giving it a voice you recognize. Try giving the voice a distinctive tone. Also look out for unusual physiological sensations that precede an intuitive insight. Your mind and your body are one; they are in harmony. If your mind fails to get your attention then your body will often try to give it a helping hand. So also be aware of odd sensations in your body that may be associated with your intuition.

Tip Developing intuition within a group requires a high degree of trust because each person's intuition may work in dissimilar ways. If working with others, try to ensure you start with a clear idea of your useful differences and learn to work synergistically.

As an example of how separation might be used, consider the interaction between two people.

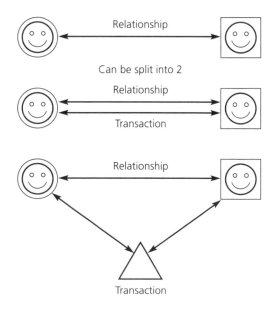

This example may look simple and logical after the fact, and it is. However, when we are thinking on our feet during a negotiation or a conflict, we can sometimes forget that several separate forces are in play. Failing to recognize these forces or misunderstanding the sequence in which they tend to play out will seriously undermine the quality of the outcome you desire.

Separation reminds us to disentangle the components and then to watch ourselves engage our thoughts at each level.

Pressured situations where we must remain effective in our thinking include a whole range of different ones, such as negotiation, conflict, influencing others and our personal relationships. The following seven principles might be useful:

1 Be entirely self-reliant within your own space.

2 Be willing to read and acknowledge the forces in play.

3 Recognize your role in the forces at work.

4 Be willing to watch yourself and to stay in control of yourself, your emotions and your thoughts.

5 Be prepared to act true to yourself, to your values and to fair principles.

6 Respond at the appropriate level.

7 Keep learning.

Let's consider as an example an adversarial confrontation between two politicians from opposed political parties. Separation allows passionate debate and prevents personal conflict arising because both parties agree to differ, even to an enormous degree, on the substance of the issue at one level, while preserving their professional relationship at another. The relationship has been separated from the transaction – in this case the debate. At the end of a very heated, passionately delivered debate, both can pick up their professional relationship or friendship at another level because this has *not* been challenged. From an onlooker's point of view this friendship may seem hypocritical. It is not. The two politicians agree to disagree in one domain while they agree to be great friends in another. They can disagree but still respect the other's position. Thinking can be improved by learning to separate relationships from transactions.

Thinking can be improved by learning to separate relationships from transactions

Thinking, feelings, expectations, motivations and behaviour are all inter-twined. If we fail to acknowledge this, then any appreciation of how we think will be stunted and dull.

So, for the sake of illustration let us continue to use the example of our two politicians and introduce a third level of transaction, namely emotion. Let's suggest that outside the debating chamber one of our politicians is young and unwittingly tramples on a deeply personal belief that enrages the emotions of the other politician. A red button has been pushed. In the immediate exchange that follows the young politician will make no progress whatsoever at the logical level.

If you are prepared to be patient, there is a sequence of approach that can be worked through that will eventually return you to a logical basis where reasonable thought can once more be rationally employed. The sequence looks like this:

- Emotions, if expressed → acknowledge the other person.
- → Stay unemotional → continue to listen and signal you acknowledge the other person's feelings (this does not mean you have to agree). Try not to damage the relationship. The other person will signal when they have moved out of the emotional phase. (Remember, though, a return to emotion may occur if feelings remain suppressed or unanswered.)
- Rapport → establish → maintain → repair → improve.
- Logic → engage the transaction(s).
- Relationship → maintain as unconditionally separate from the transaction.

Tip In business, emotions often can get pushed into the background. Emotional expression will usually be preceded by some kind of build-up signals. Being attentive to the other person and halting a logical process and reverting to addressing emotions rather than logic may help defuse a difficult situation. If you blunder on in the hope of logically talking your way out, you can forget it – you will only make matters worse. Once lit, an emotional fuse needs immediate and careful attention!

There are limits to the value of thinking. In some special relationships, more emotion and less logic is actually what is required!

> **Tip** In personal relationships, people will sometimes try to stir up emotions in other individuals they hold strong feelings for, simply to see if the other person still cares or feels in a particular way. Under these circumstances the endpoint is not about logic. The desired outcome is an emotional engagement.

There are also some situations where no amount of effort will move the transaction process into the realm of rational thought. Some people enjoy emotional situations more than others do: while some feel more in control when swimming in their favourite emotional soup, others simply do not want closure. Under these circumstances it is best simply to let go of the connections, to dispassionately disconnect, perhaps permanently, or until more reasonable behaviour replaces unacceptable social practices.

> **Tip** Never tussle with a pig – the gutter is its domain, *you* will get dirty and the pig enjoys the dirt.

> **Tip** When a conflict arises, in the initial stage drop the logic and acknowledge the other person's feelings. This does not mean you have to agree with the feelings or how they are displayed. Acknowledging the other's feelings simply shows you are aware of the other person's emotional situation. This can be done by voice and volume matching, but remain separate and do not engage your own emotions. When emotions have been dealt with, a calming period will help a return to considered thinking.

In summary

We rarely think about thinking. We may be unaware of how present knowledge gets in the way of learning new things. By developing a sense of self-awareness and an overview of our thinking we can begin to enhance the quality of the thoughts we choose. When we think, several rational and non-rational forces can come into play. In order to understand how we perform, we need to understand the order in which these forces operate. To do this we need to 'separate', to step back and to monitor our own thoughts as they occur. We also need to develop an awareness of our emotions and their role in our thinking and behaviour.

I hope that the scissors graph illuminates the futility of over-reliance on increasing amounts of hard work. Working smarter, not harder, is the way to survive and thrive within a complex future.

Building upon the ideas we have developed so far, Chapters 2 and 3 will look at two concepts that are fundamental to the quality of thinking, namely the directions our thoughts take and the frames of reference we build.

Thinking: It's so simple really – we all do it, but differently

2

Getting on the same wavelength. Checking your direction

If you are the type of reader who 'surfs' through a book reading only some of the pages, then I recommend you read these. They are central to understanding how our minds process information.

The problem I most frequently encounter with busy professionals is that most of us have a thinking pattern that is strongly biased towards one particular pattern. This particular pattern works well in some common circumstances, but actually limits us in many more.

To illustrate my meaning about how we shape our minds, I want you to create an image in your mind and to imagine yourself as a fighting crab, the type of crab that has one truly huge claw! Create an image in your mind about how the crab moves and how it carries itself. Our crab cannot do anything but lead with its one huge claw! As you think about this crab, you may find it difficult to picture where the other smaller claw is or to imagine how such an undeveloped little claw can ever be of any use.

Now imagine a brain equally lopsided. Intellectually our development tends to produce minds that are about as lopsided as the distribution of crab fighting muscle. The way we 'work out' with our brains reinforces this pattern. As a biologist, I can see why in survival terms some crabs do evolve like this. One huge claw beats two average ones in a fight every time! But what if the fighting stops and new rules are applied? The imbalance that once provided advantage becomes a liability.

I spend a good deal of time working with people from high-pressure environments and witness evidence of intellectual distortion. In the past, as a very

One huge claw beats two average ones in a fight every time!

busy manager responsible for the activity of other managers all operating under high pressure, I too have felt these distortions at first hand. Have you noticed how some people are so pressured they actually speak at more than twice the natural speaking speed used by people living at normal pace? Clearly, for people behaving like this 'doing' more equates to efficiency. Occasionally you might also notice that people are so pressured their voices sound cracked and strained. Close your eyes and what you are hearing is the voice of an elderly person. What people under this sort of pressure fail to realize is that efficiency is vastly different from effectiveness.

Yet another indication that all is not well with the shape of our minds is the tendency for people to think in sound-bites, or in smaller and smaller chunks. Their preference is for quick, easy responses allied to an aversion to reflecting, or thinking loosely, about possibilities other than *the one right answer*. This sort of behaviour will usually include an inability to relax.

All of this stress and sense of haste within a high-performance climate indicates clearly to me that our thinking abilities are being pushed to the limit. Pushing our thinking to the limit may be good for a while, but it leaves little slack for a crisis or for creative, proactive strategic thinking.

Perhaps a little time spent considering *how* we think would be useful and might help us shape up better in the future. We could re-adjust the balance of our thinking patterns and even discover ways of making work not only more effective but more fun too.

Convergent and divergent thinking

How to think is not usually taught in school. *What* to learn is certainly made clear through exam marking. But the *how* of thinking is left up to each one of us to acquire as we go along. Usually, people subconsciously adopt a preferred thinking pattern or style and stick to this for most of their lives.

So what if we could improve the thinking performance not only of individuals but also of a group? This would be a very powerful output.

Let's take a few steps back and look at the most elementary thinking patterns first. This next exercise goes some way towards explaining the two most basic thinking directions. To illustrate how unique our individual thinking is, try the following simple game with a group of friends. Each person starts with a large piece of unlined paper.

The *how* of thinking is left up to each one of us to acquire as we go along

Ask each person to consider 'fruit' and then to spend two minutes or so putting on paper what occurs to them. Then compare papers with a colleague and tot up how many things on your paper you have in common.

To the amazement of the group, you will typically find 80–90 per cent of the output is different. If two people write, say, ten words each, very few of the words will be the same. There is a *divergence* of responses.

The first of the following observations about this exercise when completed is so obvious that it is easily missed:

- Almost everyone uses words.
- Very few people express themselves in more than single words.
- Most people write neatly in columns.
- In six years of running this exercise I have not seen poetry.
- Very rarely have I witnessed people writing sentences.
- Occasionally I now see pictures as a response.

(More pictures started to appear in response to this exercise when I re-drafted the question. Instead of asking people to think about 'the *word* fruit', I now simply ask them to think about 'fruit' and to 'put' (instead of 'write') on paper whatever comes into their mind. Even with this correction, most people still choose words.)

When we see that 80–90 per cent of people's responses to the fruit exercise are so different, we can acknowledge that what we are thinking individually during a conversation is not necessarily what the person communicating with us is thinking.

Also, the way the words are laid out on the paper often tells us that our thinking and the display of our thoughts are shaped by an ingrained need to conform to a pattern laid down *by* a teacher, *for the benefit of a teacher.* Words are often laid out in list form to conserve space and for easy marking. Through our education system we have disciplined our minds to work according to a pattern that works well for people who wish to quickly grade our thinking. While the marking system in education is efficient, our learning *how to think* is not always best served by these disciplines.

> **'*What* to think' and '*what* to remember' is the old way.**
> **The new way will be *how* to think.**

Some people believe that too much educational discipline applied to very young children limits their later potential as adult thinkers. Encouraging diverse interest in music, art and creative activity in the early years is more likely to produce agile minds capable of living in a dynamic environment.

As human animals we have an instinct for patterns, images and shapes

The observation about the most common response, to hundreds of 'Fruit' exercises during many years of thinking skills workshops, being in the form of words rather than pictures, suggests to me that as a species we may be missing out somehow. We may be under-utilizing a skill that served us well in the past but which in many of us has been submerged under needs driven by a relatively recent academic process. As human animals we have an instinct for patterns, images and shapes. If today we could employ more imagery in our thinking, then we could tap into an area of our minds that helped us in the past to sense risk and opportunity. Society seems to agree that 'a picture is worth a thousand words', but so far we have not learned how to fully and, more importantly, how to *consistently* exploit the use of imagery in our thinking. This was one of the lines of thinking that gave rise to this book.

One of the reasons for the high variety of thoughts in the fruit exercise is the nature of the question itself. If we were to ask a group to consider 'the colours of fruit', that would make the task quite specific and the degree to which individuals' responses agreed would be much higher: we might expect 70–80 per cent of the responses to be the same. Asking for something specific is a *closing*-down question. The pathway is well defined and, as a consequence, the thinking consistently converges towards answers from within a more limited range of choices. In contrast, asking for 'something to do with …' is a much more *open* question that naturally leads to more possibilities. The answers to an open question tend to diverge away from each other.

> **Tip** The lesson here is that rather than immediately reacting to and answering a question, you should step back and ask yourself, 'First, do I need to reply, and second, if I do, what sort of question we are dealing with?' This approach can help you to offer your best-considered response.

Two basic patterns of thinking

The fruit exercise and the answering patterns demonstrate two fundamental patterns for thought. One is all about focus or getting down to specifics and is referred to as *convergent thinking*, while the other is its opposite and is referred to as *divergent thinking*. One style converges upon an answer, while the other moves away or diverges. A question composed to be specific or 'closed', requesting colours of fruit, produces a focused answer. However, an open, vague question produces the opposite, a divergent response.

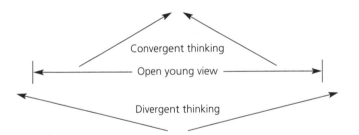

Convergent thinking is associated with focus and with closing down to definite answers. Converging upon an endpoint is a basic desire of this kind of thinking. Divergent thinking, on the other hand, is associated with exploration and creativity, with opening up and moving away.

Each of these two major pathways has a set of rules, which are diametrically opposed to each other. It is impossible to try to mix the two thinking patterns at the same time. The easiest way to frustrate thinking along either path is to use the wrong rule set. For example, 'an exploratory journey into the unknown' is a vital aspect of divergent thinking, so a demand to focus and complete the task or to 'arrive' will be deeply annoying to a divergent thinker. By contrast, imagine someone in a crisis who needs urgent specific answers and clear instructions: they would view as rash or extremely irresponsible any attempts to be creative.

We all have access to and we all use both of these two major thinking patterns to differing degrees. Convergent thinking, however, is massively rewarded in the world of work and education, while divergent thinking is much less often rewarded. We are progressively discouraged away from utilizing divergent thinking skills in education and the workplace where conformity and focus are considered essential. In this way we end up with 'fighting-crab'-like brains – totally lopsided.

There are a few, though, who excel at employing both convergent and divergent patterns of thinking. People with good social skills who are able to deploy both thinking patterns and who are also good at filtering essential data will often be selected in business and government, as leaders and decision makers. Often people with these natural skills can think at lightning speed and can be impatient because they fail to appreciate that their thinking skills advantages are not present in others.

Unfortunately for many of us, developing this dual-pattern thinking skill feels counter-intuitive. In some countries the cultural structures reinforce convergent thinking. For example, institutions and organizations are often arranged to reflect a convergent pyramidal thinking pattern: armies, the Christian church, and many business organizations all tend to have a focal point or 'head' over increasingly large sub-layers of management. This makes sense if the alignment of large numbers of people is necessary for large-scale activity such as monument building, mass production, war and education.

In some countries the cultural structures reinforce convergent thinking

Hence we are in the main encouraged by our history and our society to think in a convergent way; most of us tend to look for *the* correct answer. As a way of thinking, this has clear, decisive advantages of speed. The disadvantage of this approach, however, is that we often overlook alternatives because our predisposition to focus will unconsciously and rapidly deselect any information arriving at our senses that does not conveniently 'fit' what we expect to see.

Over centuries, there has been a relentless pressure to improve the rate at which we produce and deliver products and services, and with it the demands to focus our minds are increasing, as are the rewards for those who can do so. Many people decide to dispense with the more relaxed and chaotic divergent thinking pattern of a playful childhood in order to focus instead on living 'more successful' lives. Consequently the majority of working adults end up with focused thinking as their main drive. Men *generally* tend to be quite good at focused thinking. In evolutionary terms our industrialized society is seconds old. From an evolutionary perspective, high focus may be advantageous when a fast-hunting, live-or-die decision is required, but not in other situations. In predominantly male-controlled work environments it is unsurprising to find focused convergent thinking as the dominant thinking style determined by exemplary performers who have reached the top.

Nature likes diversity, so fortunately there are other thinking patterns that shape people's behaviour. For example, a modest number of people find they cannot live in a world of hard-driven focus. They prefer to thrive on the chaos of divergent thinking in creative enterprises or in alternative lifestyles. These men and women may be regarded as creative free spirits, sometimes outrageous or even irresponsible, by people who live in more rule-bound realities.

Then there are a small number of brilliant people who develop a synergy between convergent and divergent thinking to deliver a dazzling intellect that seems to be beyond the grasp of the rest of us. Possession of such brilliance may attract the description 'genius'.

Any original thinking requires a considerable degree of exploration and therefore divergent thinking is very important. Clearly a predominantly divergent thinker is likely to be very different.

We all possess the ability to deploy both thinking styles. The problem is we tend to operate a bias towards the one we prefer. So how might it be if we used more of our less-utilized thinking pattern?

Imagine you lived with someone who for most of the time was a convergent thinker. What would life be like? Would it be fun or dull? Could they be relied upon? Would they be a source of good ideas? If they came upon a good idea, could they be relied upon to carry it out? Now consider living with a mostly divergent thinker and ask the same questions.

Tip It may not be productive to try to have a one-size-fits-all policy on working procedures, policy and office design within organizations that wish to fully utilize people with quite different thinking skills. If you value diversity, then you may need to think about using different settings and contexts to provoke appropriate thinking. Do your meetings run only to one pattern? Effectively managing the ability to be inconsistent could become an interesting strength for organizations that value diversity.

Arriving is not the point – it's a journey

The thinking pathway used by divergent thinkers is very open, quite the opposite of the focused, convergent process. Divergent thinking moves away, outward, seeking something interesting along a journey. These journeys or departures can be very pleasurable and therefore divergent people feel unhappy or frustrated if someone stops their journey process. The way divergent thinkers deliver their ideas is via processes that will definitely feel counter-intuitive to focused thinkers and, as a consequence, people who are predominantly divergent thinkers do not often fit in easily within companies or large structured organizations. Divergent thinkers tend to see focused thinkers as narrow minded and far too short term, while their more focused colleagues see them as irritatingly unfocused, even butterfly minded or feather brained.

Let me illustrate how the difference of thinking direction can cause problems. I once asked an artist friend of mine a very unfair question: 'Who is your favourite artist?' A simple enough question to a focused person, but one that is extremely unreasonable from the perspective of a divergent thinker. The question caused visible discomfort as she struggled to rationalize so many interesting facets of so many different domains of art over several centuries down to just one choice. The question almost stalled her thinking! How could someone narrow down so much art to one person? When she realized the question was unfair (to her), she replied to the nature of the question and not the content of the question itself.

This illustrates that to get the most out of a good divergent thinker, you must ask the right sort of questions and, importantly, be prepared and open to their type of response. You must also provide a divergent thinker with time to reflect, and when they reply you should try to be 'open' to what they 'suggest'. Often, divergent thinkers may find focused answers as repugnant as focused questions. Answers from good divergent thinkers may require further consideration by focused thinkers. If anything, a good divergent thinker will stretch your horizons and make you begin to think about interesting questions you had not yet considered. When under pressure, however, focused thinkers will find it saves time and is easier to ask a like-minded focused thinker for a quick answer, though the quality of the response is not going to be anywhere near as interesting!

> **To get the most out of a good divergent thinker, you must ask the right sort of questions**

A creative mind is more likely to provide an exciting clue than a specific answer. Also the thinking tools a divergent thinker may employ are likely to be elastic and flexible. For example, a divergent thinker may be quite comfortable using generalizations when facts are non-existent, vague or loose.

Generalization: A divergent thinking tool

Generalization is an old, previously common tool that I use. As with any tool, poor use leads to poor results. Used blindly, a generalization is a tool that can be used to misrepresent or to wrongly bias an argument. Used with conscious awareness, though, a generalization remains a useful tool in indicating a direction or the outline of an embryonic concept. Generalizing is a useful tool so long as we remember it indicates a degree of elasticity within the area under discussion. Generalizations only ever indicate a partial truth (see Chapter 9). A generalization is never absolutely true and at best is only a rough approximation. In order to emphasize we are *consciously* using a very crude thinking tool, I have used the term 'generally' in italics throughout the book.

A generalization has intrinsic limitations. This does not suggest we should stop using this useful tool. People may feel reluctant to generalize for a variety of reasons. Generalization is risky because someone may oppose your interpretation or someone else may demand to see extensive research that proves the point in absolute terms. Sometimes generalizations are dangerous because they come up against arbitrary views and meet with rigid thinking head on. Unfortunately the use of generalization as a tool has been curtailed by the assumption that generalizations are *always* dangerous and that scientific analysis is *always* to be preferred (see Chapter 3 on good and bad assumptions). I believe this sort of rigidity is at least as dangerous as a bad generalization and an unreasonable limitation on thinking.

There are realms of thinking where structured logic work best and others where more elastic thinking can pay dividends. Convergent thinking favours logical approaches and divergent patterns tolerate open-ended thinking and creativity. In between these two areas is a territory where thinking deals in terms of generalization, ambiguity and synthesis (see Chapters 5, 8 and 11). As we mature we must learn to work in all three thinking areas or, if we cannot, then we should learn how to work effectively with people who can complement our own thinking abilities so that we can work smarter.

The direction our thinking takes has a material impact on behaviour and upon problem solving, as can be seen in the following shopping inset.

Thinking patterns and shopping

When I go shopping for shoes, I know exactly which shop to go to. I am certain of the colour and brand I want, and I'm ready to pay, within reasonable limits, what I have paid previously. My mission accomplished, I quickly leave and do something more interesting than shopping. Basically, I don't enjoy it. My shopping style is mostly about mission, focus and result. This is clearly a convergent thinking and equally convergent behaviour pattern. I rationalize my behaviour as 'not wasting time'.

Contrast this with the behaviour of one of my friends when shopping for shoes. She prefers to look at as many shoes, in as many shops, as possible. Acquiring the shoes is actually secondary to the real aim, which is to have a really good look around! The pleasure is in the looking, the exploring, not necessarily in the acquiring. In that sense this behaviour is divergent. Buying the shoes would mean stopping the enjoyment of looking around. Even if the ideal pair of shoes was in the first shop, I should not expect our journey to end there. Carefully checking all the available territory seems to be very important. She would rationalize her behaviour as making sure she had not missed a better pair in another shop.

If I tried (and I have) to reason that we should use my preferred shoe-buying pattern, what sort of reaction would you expect? Conflict! If not conflict, then a deep sense of frustration because my preference is likely to spoil my friend's shopping pattern just as much as her preference for looking around will frustrate any mission-minded person like me.

I should point out that I have some women friends who shop in a focused way and some male friends who enjoy the browsing approach. Also when we change the product to say something hi-tech, a quite different shopping pattern emerges. The point of the anecdote is not gender differentiation but to give a memorable way of illustrating how our preferred patterns of thinking shape how we behave. (The retail world, incidentally, figured this pattern of thinking and behaviour out decades ago and now arranges its product displays to match the most likely behaviours of its preferred customers.)

Our preferences for divergent and convergent patterns of thinking have important implications for the way that we talk to each other, the way we attempt to help each other, the way that we relate to each other during a discussion and the way that we argue during a conflict.

Patterns of thinking and problem resolution

The way we think and the way patterns sometimes engage automatically can be seen in the patterns *generally* adopted by small groups of men compared to small groups of women. It is important that we notice the difference in the two patterns, irrespective of the gender, because a failure to recognize our own patterns can cause unnecessary communication difficulties.

When faced with a problem within a small group, men will tend to make statements such as 'What you need to do is …' or 'Why not do this …?', which are based on results and solution. Their problem-solving orientation is about focus and is biased strongly toward a solution or a result. Early closure and moving on are important. Reflection is often minimal, sentences short. It would not be unusual for someone to change the subject completely. This is very much a one-stage, action-orientated process.

Small groups of women, by contrast, will *generally* adopt quite a different approach. They will tend to 'share' a problem and will pose open questions. Their aim is to help the problem owner look around the territory, to uncover lots of possibilities, not necessarily to provide a resolution to the problem but to offer support along the journey and to open up new avenues of enquiry. It is a two-stage process.

Both problem-solving approaches are employed by all of us at different times. However we do seem to have a 'default' problem-solving pattern that we employ without conscious awareness. The essential point is that if we fail to spot which styles are in operation, we can easily end up with unnecessary misunderstandings and poor communication.

Imagine mixing these two styles and that two people, in this example a man and a woman, wish to solve a problem. For the sake of illustration let's also assume a man adopts the convergent, quick-answer style and a woman adopts a desire for a more rounded, divergent problem-solving approach. The outcome is unlikely to be productive. He will no doubt express a frustration such as, 'She's not listening. I offered three perfectly good solutions and none of them seems good enough!' From

▶

the divergent thinker's point of view, concern would be expressed in a more open statement such as, 'But you don't understand ...'.

So what is happening here? In essence, it is probable that the person using a convergent pattern may actually have made quite useful contributions from a focusing perspective, but their offers are not timely or appropriate because they closed down the discovery process of exploring all the territory. Only when all the stones have been turned over and looked at will a person adopting a divergent problem-solving pattern feel ready to select their option for action.

Both problem-solving approaches, irrespective of gender, have their merits. In a crisis or when time is short, a thinking process that leads to early action may be preferable whereas, when a well-considered approach is needed, the two-stage divergent pattern to find options followed by a decision would work best. The problem is that we are rarely aware of the pattern we are deploying and in conversation we rarely tell others about the route our minds are taking.

Tip If you are more used to following a closing pattern, try being more patient with yourself and others; take time to reflect; don't close so quickly and try to remain open. Try not to offer specifics unless asked. If you want responses to your problem to follow an open, exploratory pattern, guide the other person on what you actually want now – either assistance to look around or, when appropriate, three clear solutions.

The two natural patterns in their pure form do not mix at all well together. One is narrow and specific, the other broad and considered. One pattern can be too narrow-minded, just as the other has the potential to confuse people and carries a risk for the problem owner of getting lost in their own muddled maze of alternatives. Even when the alternatives are clear, a decision may still not be forthcoming, perhaps because an advantage is sensed in *not* deciding and keeping the options or the process open.

At work it will become increasingly important to recognize which patterns are being deployed and to what end.

Thinking styles at work

The advantages of the focused employee tend to be obvious. They are results orientated and they work wonderfully when the work they are doing 'fits' the current paradigm. Focused thinkers are likely to be able to track each other relatively easily, once everyone understands what to focus on.

The benefit of using the good divergent thinkers is they are often excellent at generating ideas and alternatives. The trouble is, they don't always enjoy finishing something, nor do they tend to work comfortably within a disciplined system! Divergent thinkers, by their nature, may find other divergent thinkers difficult to track, so working with such a group may feel chaotic.

There are people who were born 'brilliant' and then there are remarkable people who have been lucky enough to have learned early in life how to master how to employ both convergent *and* divergent skills. Often these appear to us as intuitive entrepreneurs, innovators or charismatic leaders with great vision, or as geniuses. Alternatively they can make remarkable managers, who seem to be able to sort out the most complex multifaceted issues more quickly than average. The good news is that both patterns can be learned or enhanced at any age.

So, does having a simple map of the intellectual process mean we can all learn how to be a genius in a workshop or on a course? In a word, no; moreover the evidence shows that, while the thinking skills can be acquired, it can take ten years of hard work to realize truly inspiring, illuminating work that might be classified as 'brilliant' in the arts and sciences. So developing the thinking patterns that are intuitively employed by a genius will not turn you into a brilliant performer overnight. The good news is that, once you recognize that there are two quite distinct thinking patterns, both can be developed to steadily improve thinking performance in you and your colleagues.

Tip Are you often frustrated by the slowness of others to see solutions as fast as you do? Do you have a senior manager who is like this? In both cases the communication gap can be bridged by understanding that others do not have similar thinking patterns. I have seen very high-performance managers fall early because they were unable to 'inclusively lead' towards a clear goal. A lack of understanding of others' abilities may manifest itself as a lack of empathy or a lack of sympathy for others who cannot think fast.

Intellectual mobility

The ability to master both convergent and divergent thinking, together with an ability to 'see' or to visualize connections between previously unconnected ideas, is the basis of potential genius. Higher thinking ability depends on intellectual agility, flexibility, capacity and depth of experience. In my experience, women *generally* are more familiar and comfortable using their divergent thinking skills than men are. Men are *generally* thought to be good at aggressive, tenacious, single-minded activity, whereas women *generally* are often better at multitasking. As future work becomes more complex, this observation could have major implications in the world of work. One of the most complex types of decision making that requires multitasking is flying a combat aircraft. So far this is a male preserve. As military aircraft become more complex, perhaps in the future women rather than men will be more likely to pass the aptitude and performance tests required for managing multiple avionics and weapons systems.

> **As military aircraft become more complex, perhaps in the future women rather than men will be more likely to pass the aptitude and performance tests**

Business is not getting any simpler, is it? So how is the personnel selection process going to be different in the future to reflect these changing demands?

Because women are naturally inclined to use both convergent and divergent thinking I believe women *generally* may have an advantage over the average male in a fast-changing complex world. Where male-type brains may, on the other hand, have an advantage over female-type brains is in the ability to rotate imagery in three dimensions in their mind and *generally* to be more aggressive and able to exclusively focus.

Turning now to the issue of developing a form of leadership, there are two major options for overcoming the potential confusion created within groups of managers and executives with passionately held conflicting views. Either one person has an exceptionally clear, strong-minded view and others follow out of fear or respect *or* a small, tightly knit, complementary, well-aligned team works employing creative conflict to arrive at high-quality decisions. As the world of business becomes more complex, it becomes increasingly rare for any one individual to possess the ability or the capacity to make and take all the major decisions at a consistently high level of quality. Individuals who do possess this ability will command a premium from organizations that depend upon or need this sort of leadership. Where speed becomes paramount or when faced with a major dilemma, teams may yield to the ancient Roman idea of rule by 'diktat', where in a crisis one person was given absolute power.

In theory the most powerful combination should be small, tightly knit groups of convergent and divergent thinkers. Each would possess different but complementary skills and the group would intuitively know and trust each other's judgement. Developing collective thinking skills takes time because trust building takes time. One of the keys to the success of this sort of shared power is the speed of decision making and implementation.

You may notice I only use a few quotations in this book. However, this one caught my eye:

> Man is a fighting animal; his thoughts are his banners and it is a failure of nerve in him if they are only thoughts.
>
> GEORGE SANTAYANA, *DIALOGUES IN LIMBO*, 1925

In the near future, as the amount of knowledge available outstrips the average person's ability to remember even a reasonable portion of it, intellectual mobility and the ability to act decisively will probably become more important than exam-passing ability. For those of us who will be faced with increasingly complex demands, our future well-being will be a question of how well we balance those of our personal lives with those of work. In working smarter, as opposed to harder, achieving a balance will require our students and managers to learn new ways of preparing and exercising their minds. Increasing proficiency in forming intelligent patterns, shaping meaning from new information or generating original thought will be more valuable within information-rich environments, especially where computer memory and processing power become exponentially cheaper. Building mental muscle will therefore be just as much a question of improved performance at work as attaining a sense of well-being.

Exercise and make the most of what you have

If we all did body-building exercises, the varied outcomes would be the product of an amalgam of how much effort we put in and of our unique starting material. We can all improve our physical fitness through exercise, some more than others. Likewise we can all improve our minds. The sport-shoe manufacturer Nike's 20th-century advertising concept of 'No pain, no gain' applies to the world of a creative genius too. Exercising 'mental muscle' can improve anyone, given sufficient practice.

The sport-shoe manufacturer Nike's 20th-century advertising concept of 'No pain, no gain' applies to the world of a creative genius too

If we are to remain healthy and effective within our employment in the 21st century, we will all have to acknowledge our potential for intellectual imbalance. There are healthy thinking habits just as there are healthy eating and exercise habits. Developing self-awareness of our thinking is the first step.

The value in understanding the two basic ways of thinking is that each one of us can adopt them in a determined way to generate either original, novel solutions or focused, determined responses. Difficulties can be overcome more imaginatively. With practice, competitive advantage can be realized in the world of work or progress in your career improved. With patience, more effective solutions can be found to resolve our personal problems.

> **Tip** When it comes to the quality of thinking, patience is a worthy virtue. Some of our thoughts require time to incubate. Having time to reflect is essential to the quality of what we think. Practising being patient with your own thoughts will pay dividends. As you become more patient with yourself, you may find you become patient with others too.

As we begin to learn how to stimulate and gain access to under-utilized thinking abilities and to become more at ease with 'open' divergent creativity, synthesis and holistic thinking, we will create a pleasant counter-balance against high pressure and high focus. We may even end up happier!

In summary

We can make improvements in the way we think by developing a practical awareness of the two fundamental directions that our thoughts can take, namely convergent and divergent thinking. In a world where focus is heavily emphasized, a limiting factor for many people is their inability to use divergent thinking effectively. In addition, what is missing from many people's thinking repertoires are simple models, maps and tools.

High-performance people seem to be able to draw upon a variety of intellectual resources. Their rapid problem-solving ability or incisive analysis of where the key business issues are suggests they move quickly through divergent thinking and then focus using convergent thinking.

Often high-performance people's thinking will exist within some form of patterns or models that consistently work for them: they will describe shapes in the air with their hands to describe how they 'see' the situation.

Once people understand the two fundamental directions and how to use them, holistic thinking can start to add value. Add a kit-bag of thinking tools and the scope and quality of someone's thinking can be improved with practice. With this in mind we will look at a variety of models and aids to thinking in subsequent chapters.

Having considered the convergent and divergent paths along which we may travel, we now need to consider how we perceive the world. The way each of us perceives the world is unique and highly personal. We each possess a uniquely personal sense of reality that is viewed through our personalized mind's-eye lenses, or frames of reference. These frames of reference shape our expectations and our aspirations.

If we fail to be aware or to understand what these forces are, we cannot expect to influence them. The next chapter explains why an understanding of our frames of reference is the next essential step in understanding and developing improved thinking skills.

Frames of reference 3

Frames of reference are fundamentally important because most of our thoughts are channelled and shaped by them. Frames keep us healthy by helping us to conserve energy and by allowing us to reduce the anxiety we feel when confronted with the unknown. We are mostly unaware of them. Frames of reference work in the background, behind our conscious thinking processes.

To help us visualize a frame of reference, imagine a picture frame and because the most common picture frames are rectangular, we will use this particular shape in the rest of the book. Often we look at the picture within the frame but rarely spend time considering the construction or function of the frame itself. Frames of reference, like picture frames, do have a vital role in our thinking.

Frames of reference shape how we make sense of the world around us. The same information viewed by different people using different frames of reference will be perceived quite differently. Let's consider how frames of reference are built up.

A frame of reference is, in simple terms, a linked collection of beliefs we hold in our thoughts about what we believe to be real, true, fixed and certain. We tend not to be aware of this part of our perception unless specific attention is drawn toward it, usually when our thinking faces a major challenge.

When we begin to consider the 'facts and truths' in our lives, we do not at first see them for what they often are, namely assumptions or relative truths and often partial truths. Once set in place, these assumptions form the foundations of our frames of reference and are only rarely checked or

Frames of reference

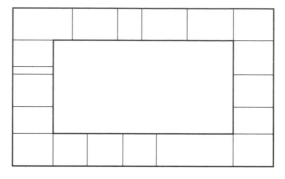

re-evaluated. Frames are extremely useful in many everyday situations; however, the assumptions can become a primary weakness in our thinking.

A frame of reference captures all sorts of knowledge that builds up to our own unique personalized picture of a subject or issue. Everything we know about an issue hangs upon and within a particular framework. These frameworks are designed to speed up the way we deal with familiar subjects.

Frames need not be static: they can and do change with new experience. They tend to be added to, in supporting layers. Unlike picture frames, a frame of reference is a composition of many different elements. Each element may contain all sorts of sensations, images, feelings, impressions and ideas.

Everybody has many little interlinked frames of reference, but we all have one larger frame about who we are, and our place within life's bigger picture. These bigger self-image frames of reference are fundamental to our individual sense of well-being. Your big picture is painted within this frame and much of the artistry is in your own hands.

As an example of the dynamic changing nature of our frames of reference, consider a time when you had to face up to something that you believed important, but of which you had little or no experience. For many people, thinking about the first time they took control of a car or a motor bike conjures up vivid memories of the level of anxiety *and* at the same

Your big picture is painted within this frame and much of the artistry is in your own hands

time the sense of exhilaration at taking control of an expensive and potentially lethal, but exciting machine. Memories of this early experience may seem vivid relative to other experiences and may include tactile information plus peculiar sounds and smells. If you are a driver, try to recall your memory of this event. When you recall this memory, remember the thoughts and feelings you had at the time. You will see that the strong memories come back to you with 'attachments' such as associated smells, images and feelings – which is why they last so well.

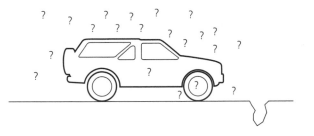

When you reflect upon that experience, you will remember you had many unanswered questions in your mind. What were the other drivers going to do? How would you react if a lamp-post suddenly 'jumped out' in front of you? These and many other unanswered questions may have filled your mind. Your attention was heightened. In the absence of any reassuring certainties, you were on full body alert to any unknown dangers. And then there was the thrill of completing the journey, and being able to say confidently that you had begun something new. Many people also recall that at the end of the driving lesson they were exhausted. Huge amounts of thinking energy are needed to maintain us at such states of heightened awareness. Just imagine always living at this sort of energy level. Life would be frenetic, important, dramatic, vivid – but quite short! We would simply burn out both emotionally and biologically.

The reason we expend so much mental energy when faced with novelty is that we place an extreme demand on our mind to quickly capture enough new information to render the novelty down to useful behaviour, or to dismiss a real and present threat. In the car example we try to get hold of everything we need to know about 'car'. We do this so that we can acquire certainty about something perceived as important to us. We tend not to be aware of how we are processing our thoughts about the new information; we remain unaware of how we are driven towards certain goals. What happens in our minds is that we build up a new frame of reference that gradually fills up with all the experiences we need to competently use a car. As the certainty increases with more, repeated, confirmed, patterned information the anxiety decreases as we become progressively more confident that we can predict what will happen to us when we drive.

Your experience allows your mind to drive on auto-pilot

Contrast the last time you drove your car – now, as a mature driver – with the first. These two acts could not be more different because by now you have automated much of what happens when driving. The thinking and behaviour automation is made possible by your frame of reference; your experience allows your mind to drive on auto-pilot. Recently I shared this example with a group of managers in Cairo, Egypt. I said that perhaps I should make an exception in the case of everyday driving in Cairo! To me as a visitor, a trip across the city felt as if every car driver was riding for their very life in a Formula One race. The group laughed and said, 'No, it's normal! We get used to it.' In other words, we have a frame of reference in which we consider local conditions as 'normal'.

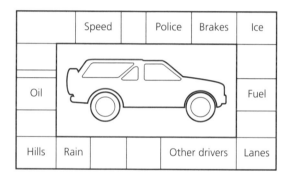

Once we are experienced in driving, previously unknown quantities, such as questions about the roads, people's behaviour in and out of cars, the other vehicles, have been mostly answered – even in Cairo, Calcutta, Milan and New York! The frame of reference depicted above shows how our thoughts surround what was once a novelty with secure information. Hence each little 'box' or sub-frame might be filled with information on hill starts, things to do with gear changes, other drivers, and so on.

Experience has now completely framed 'driving' within a series of linked, recognizable, known sub-routines.

Once these are in place, you feel at liberty to focus your available thinking attention on more interesting things. In effect you have by now automated most aspects of routine driving. Your subconscious mind can now take care of driving and, because the routines are known, you can transact them very much faster than a novice can.

Change and frames of reference

To understand the broad impact and fundamental impact of frames of reference in our thinking at work or in our social lives, consider the first time you fell in love. Wasn't it wonderful! Something magical was added to life.

When we fall in love, our own big picture initially includes a highly significant but unspoken assumption that the relationship with the other person will be 'forever'. Some people do go on to spend the rest of their lives with their first love; however, many of us get to experience the deep sense of loss that comes with the ending of our first love relationship. Our sense of 'reality' is disrupted. Where we once felt certain, secure or complete a huge gap appears. People articulate the sudden gap in their life in a physical or structural way, using phrases like 'The roof caved in on my world'.

This same pattern is acted out in our work lives when we face fundamental change. Fundamental assumptions deeply embedded in our frames of reference are knocked down or removed.

Frames of reference

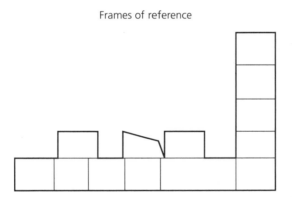

The same sense of the world collapsing as happens with the loss of love can also happen with the closing of a department. When anything we regard as secure within our frame of reference is changed or removed we feel genuine pain. Back or joint pains, or stomach disorders, can be outward signs of inner pain.

In our work lives we carry around some really large assumptions. Challenge someone's expectations to do with promotion, authority, power and influence, their social standing or what other people think of them and you'll quickly find a number of 'red buttons'; press one of these and a reaction will follow.

Recognizing the importance of deeply held assumptions within frames of reference is important. Essentially the same pattern of feeling and thinking recurs when we divorce, undergo a bereavement or face major change initiatives at work. The job of understanding and managing the resistance that accompanies such changes should be less difficult if you appreciate the intensity of such feelings. When a work frame of reference changes, this has an impact on almost everyone in an organization. For example, we know we have to take care of people who are made redundant, but we can also predict that survivors need to be taken care of too.

Many people will experience major change in their lives, particularly in their work in the shape of major restructuring. Each and every process transaction you can think of will probably exist within some form of frame of reference. Some of these frames will be incidental while others will be deeply important. In the never-ending search for efficiency, it is probable that during your career you will either be involved in driving through significant change or will feel its consequences.

Suffice to say we all have some frames of reference that profoundly affect our thoughts and shape how we sense the world. Tinkering with your own or someone else's frame of reference may have unforeseen consequences. What may seem trivial to one person may be seen as vital by someone else; for example an object, or a person's participation in some activity, might represent the outward manifestation of their status. Simple objects or rights such as carpet colours, chair types or car parking often adopt meanings beyond reason. Mess with these and you can expect irrational responses.

As an example of going against a frame of reference, I once worked very briefly with one big organization. I messed with my frame of reference by talking myself into working with people who did not have my values. Rationally speaking it was a good, well-paid job with a professional peer group doing interesting work. However, what should have been win–win very quickly turned sour when I discovered that their environment and behaviours were significantly at odds with my own frame of reference. In two days I had a very uncomfortable feeling about their attitudes and beliefs and after only four days I quit. It was unavoidable. It was an irrational move, but the right one for me. While briefly traumatic, this was another great learning event for me. My reference points about what I will and will not accept in my one life were given a much higher sense of precision.

> **Simple objects or rights such as carpet colours, chair types or car parking often adopt meanings beyond reason**

Everything we perceive, we file away in our minds in a context *relative* to something else. Within our minds we develop useful patterns that we might need later. They form the basis of our judgement. Our unique experience, our ideas and thoughts become integral parts of the frames of reference that feed our habits.

Frame it

Our thinking is shaped by information, assumptions, ideas and values embedded in the boundaries of our uniquely composed frames of reference. Frames allow us to automate and speed up the rate at which we transact everyday activities and thoughts. These sub-routines give us high speed of performance. 'Experience' is basically lots of valuable pre-set sub-routines. Speed is achieved in an unconscious automated way.

Inside the frame

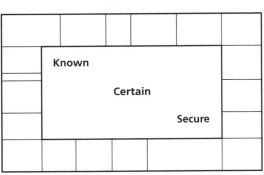

Frames provide us with a sense of certainty and security. Much less mental energy is expended when we use these sub-routines. When we are employing our frames of reference our intellectual focus can be directed elsewhere. Inside the frame decisions can be made extremely quickly.

Beyond the frames of reference

Being outside the frame of reference can be either scary or exciting, depending on your individual perception. Beyond a frame of reference, information, ideas and concepts are incomplete, partial and vague. In this outer space ideas or truths might be thought of as vapours that have not yet condensed into recognizable forms. Nothing in this area is a fact. Facts exist *relative* to something else. In this space, information, concepts and ideas are often too loose to be rationally described as facts. Only by employing imagination can our thinking find interesting possibilities in this area. High-performance people who deal with strategy, risk or big change work in this space. This is a space in which strategic thinking attempts to make sense of unformed patterns. This is also the place where innovation begins.

Frames can be a trap!

The advantages of frames of reference can quickly become a disadvantage. In terms of the way we think, a good habit differs little from a bad habit. Both are automatic thought processes that lead to predetermined patterns of behaviour requiring little or no active conscious thought.

> **In terms of the way we think, a good habit differs little from a bad habit**

Our personal frames of reference can selectively dismiss information that does not fit a recognized pattern. Therefore, if we are presented with a new opportunity or an unusual threat, we may fail to recognize it as such. In addition your frame of reference will be set within a bigger outer context for which there will be another set of rules and patterns. If this outer context in which we exist suddenly changes, our personal frames of reference may not be able to 'see' the changes coming.

In order to use your mind effectively, you need to be consciously aware of your own patterns and especially of the assumptions that make up the frame of reference in your life.

Parallel error

Frames are automated systems and, if we are not capable of over-riding them, we can become blind to information that fails to fit a pre-set pattern within our present frames' belief system. We may actually witness novel information, but we may process this new information in totally the wrong way. Orienteering runners will be familiar with the concept of parallel error. Parallel error happens in our decision-making processes when we make information fit the wrong way into something we believe to be true when it is actually false.

> **Tip** To overcome blindside errors, use independent eyes. Alarm
> bells should ring in your head when independent advice tells you
> the opposite of what you expected. To this end, always avoid 'yes'
> men and make sure your checking system includes people who
> are comfortable with conflict and who are likely to have
> alternative viewpoints. The key, though, is within you. To what
> extent are you open?

Escape the frame

It is necessary to look beyond current frames of reference if you wish to engage in strategic planning, new product or new business development, any kind of negotiation or indeed any activity requiring creativity.

One of the reasons we looked at the difference between convergent and divergent thinking patterns is that divergent thinking provides us with the necessary escape mechanism. The great news is that, with a little training, we can all learn how to escape the confines of our frames of reference or, as some would say, 'to think out of the box'.

In the diagram below, the arrows indicate different lines of thinking that diverge away from and escape the frame of reference.

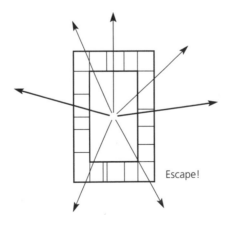

Escape!

The diagram shows us that we can cross the boundaries in many different places. For more on *how* to do this, see Chapter 11 on creative thinking tools.

Frames float around

People's frames of reference are dynamic in that they move in time relative to one another.

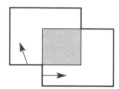

Sometimes they can break apart or be supplanted by another. This floating model is useful in various areas of business including:

- negotiating
- professional relationships
- brand positioning
- strategy
- organizational development
- PR.

There are many other applications for this simple thinking tool. Below are just two examples of how you might deploy 'frames' as a way of thinking, in these cases about negotiation and relationships at work.

Example 1: Negotiating

Frames of reference help us relate to different situations and different people. What we learn about life guides us in future interactions. One of the most complex tasks we have to face as human beings is relating to other people, especially so in a negotiation. Everyone should know how to negotiate. Negotiation skills are absolutely central to being effective because in many work situations demand for resources will often exceed availability. Negotiating how resources are shared effectively is therefore very important.

Everyone should know how to negotiate

Think about the bigger picture before you indulge the detail. This approach may help you consider what is and is not relevant and can help you think through the possibilities. Thinking in this way may also help you to select and sequence your initial activities.

The frames below show there is common ground in the overlap where two people's interests coincide or when two different groups of interests meet. At the same time we can see how each has areas in its reality where there is absolutely no commonality. A positive or negative outcome will depend on the relative positions either side adopts in this picture. If either side moves into the outer areas, progress will falter. The discussion will move away from resolution and towards position taking.

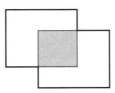

If the two sides work at fully understanding each other's frame, then both are in a significantly better starting position. Hopefully each will learn where the necessary compromises are and where the common ground might be found.

Good negotiations often hinge on how well each side is prepared to suspend judgement, i.e. old frames, long enough to search for new, bigger, better ones. In most negotiating circumstances, being able to be patiently creative can be extremely valuable. To this end, a period working outside the existing frameworks will be productive. Operating outside the boundaries will feel unfamiliar and uncomfortable for a while until new ideas emerge.

Sometimes negotiation may begin with very little or no common ground. Imagine the picture we have created of two frames overlapping to represent a relationship or a negotiation.

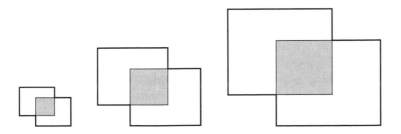

The size of the picture could be small and narrow but, by the use of our imagination, the whole scope of the negotiation could expand and become a much bigger picture. Creative activity may not necessarily

Negotiation comes down to a search for mutual benefit and then sharing or dividing up a pie

resolve all the difficulties and harmonize all the needs. However, if new thinking produces a bigger overall opportunity, then this might be regarded as progress.

Negotiation comes down to a search for mutual benefit and then sharing or dividing up a pie. The simple overlap model allows us to 'see' the consequences of the way we conduct a negotiation.

Competitive, wilful or hard-bargaining negotiations usually produce one-sided benefits and close down the search for new territory, with the inevitable result of a progressively smaller 'pie' to divide up. A search for common ground and for mutual benefit by searching for new options can create a more robust, larger and much tastier 'pie'.

> **Tip** When you are thinking about a negotiation, think big picture first and try to get a measure of how much overlap you believe you have – then try to imagine the view from the other side! Your map of how much overlap there is may be quite different from that perceived by the other person or group with whom you are negotiating. Try to put your mind inside their frame of reference. Think how they think. If the negotiation is important, try using professional actors to 'live' out the parts during your preparatory phase.

Example 2: Thinking about professional relationships

A professional relationship might be represented by two frames and their degree of overlap. See the three diagrams below: 'Reid's Relativity'. Over time, more common ground is found, indicated by the increasing overlap between the frames, and the shared relationship is enhanced.

Reid's Relativity

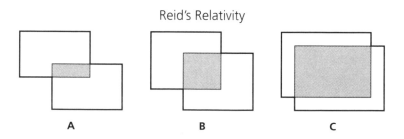

A   B   C

In some cases there may be little or no common ground, as can be seen where the two frames barely overlap. It is rare for two people to completely share the same frame of reference, i.e. have a total overlap. In other words, we will always have areas of opinion where there will be *no* common ground with people that we are close to. As a consequence, we must always expect a potential for disagreement and even conflict.

Also there is the potential for misunderstanding about the nature of the relationship itself. You may believe that the characteristics of your relationship are as in 'C', but the other person thinks of your relationship as illustrated by 'A'.

> **Tip** Think about what your agenda for interaction will be. Do you wish to generate more overlap, work within the existing overlap, move away from the other person or engage in positive conflict to reset some of the boundaries?

Positive conflict

We can all benefit from conflict when we know what the rules are

In some people there is a deep dislike of conflict and they try to avoid it at all costs. This approach to conflict may limit thinking. Therefore try to remain open to the positive opportunities of conflict with people you relate to. Conflict need not be regarded as negative. Executive board discussions are characterized by high levels of *productive* conflict. We can all benefit from conflict when we know what the rules are. Conflict can be positive if used to create better options and wiser choices.

We need not always think and operate in the area of common ground. Conflict can drive both parties to find new mutually beneficial territory.

> **Tip** Conflict is an important part of working life, so if you feel uncomfortable with it, seek out lessons in how to conduct good conflict for you and your colleagues.

> **Tip** The clarity and quality of what we think during a conflict may be compromised by emotional imbalances and by preconceptions about conflict. With this in mind, seek ways and means of dealing effectively with interpersonal conflict.

One must not overlook the fact that each person has a space where they have no commonality with others. Without differences of opinion there is little diversity of thinking and significantly less creative tension between people. Creative tension is useful some of the time, but we also need to know how and where we can compromise when required to. It is worth getting to know about and attaching value to areas you and your colleagues disagree on.

> **Tip** It is essential to remember that, in all relationships over time, each side's personal frame of reference can and will migrate, sometimes in different directions from your own. Periodically review your assumptions about your relationships.

In our relationships we do not always make explicit what our expectations and assumptions are and, while it may be considered as common sense, we often fail to recheck the assumptions and expectations of *both* sides. Do you know what your common ground is today with your boss, your company, your colleagues or your partner? We sign up to maintenance agreements on washing machines, heating systems, cars, lawnmowers – so why not relationships?

Perception

Reality is perception

Over time we build up many frames of reference that tend to make our life more comfortable and less risky. Each frame of reference turns into a quick, ready-to-use set of rules or routines. Our frames become ready-made mind's-eye lenses through which we can rapidly scan the world.

These mind's-eye lenses can be extremely helpful and may serve us exceptionally well over many years. Frames can also be a huge hindrance. Our frames of reference can actually stop us from seeing the true picture in front of us.

I married at quite a young age and had a honeymoon in Paris. Paris was pure magic in early April, so the phrase in the next diagram always rings a bell in my head!

We often see what we expect to see. If you haven't seen what's wrong with the diagram, look again. Usually about a third of a group of people,

and I am one of them, will miss the word duplicated within the triangle. Our minds'-eye lens shapes what we see based upon what we *expect*. We see and dismiss quickly because we are not actually looking: we are pattern scanning. Our ability to predict prevents a clear perception of what is actually in front of us. In one way or another all of us will have occasional blind spots caused by our mind's pattern-seeking, predictive habit.

Tip If your thinking style is that of a pattern scanner, ensure you pair up with someone who is a detail spotter. Find ways of legitimately getting a colleague with an eye for detail to regularly check your important material. If this sort of person is not available to you, try improving being 'here and now, in the moment' (see Chapter 4). On a practical level, if the material is familiar and likely to contain omissions or errors, find ways of reading the material that force you to see it as unique or unusual.

In order to truly see what is in front of us, we occasionally have to disengage our preconceptions and to ignore the well-formed mind's-eye lens long enough to actually see clearly. For a while, this means holding back an urge to decide now – being open will require you to close down any other intrusive thought process and suspend any form of judgement. Suspension might mean stopping ourselves acting in a usual or familiar way.

Being open will require you to close down any other intrusive thought process and suspend any form of judgement

We only see when we truly look

One of the skills two artist friends of mine keep stressing is 'Look, really … really look'. How can we do that with a lens in the way that predetermines what we see? 'Practise,' they both reply, adding, 'What you are looking at has got to be important.' I look, but still I do not see everything. Clearly these lenses are difficult to override. Just as our perception of the surplus

Tip One trick artists use is to turn an image upside down. This presents the eye with novel shapes and fewer triggers for preconceptions. Hence, finding a way of turning a situation on its head may present us with an opportunity to perceive new possibilities, to look with new eyes. One way to help people to 'turn things on their heads' is to solve problems employing an analogy. Find an analogy to your problem (preferably an amusing one), solve the analogous problem, then apply the solutions back to the original.

words in the Paris exercise was biased by what we thought we saw, the same fixed mind's-eye lens hinders or corrupts the shapes we think we see.

Take another example of how our mind's-eye lens shapes what we see. Consider the impression we build up of someone who in our first meetings appears to be accident prone or hostile or unhelpful. It may take only a few incidents to form a 'concrete' view about that person and what they are worth, and where they fit in our overall perception of the scheme of things. They are pigeonholed, classified and for all intents and purposes not thought about in any new contexts. In many ways such a person is literally 'forgotten', because our assumptions presume to know all there is to know about them. From then on, it takes a conscious and deliberate effort to reframe what you think you are hearing and what you believe you are seeing relative to that person. As proof, remember those people who have become remarkable success stories after they left an organization where they were not perceived as valuable.

Tip Try hard to look anew at someone you know well. Try to think about them in a new light. For example, try to get them to volunteer something about their life that would surprise you and listen as if you had never met them before. Make an effort to view them in a totally new light.

Tip With highly familiar situations, try to find a new, fresh way of viewing the component parts and try to discover something about yourself or the situation that you did not know. How could the familiar become unfamiliar, and therefore gain more of your attention?

To disengage these fixed mind's-eye lenses, these well-formed frames, is to acknowledge uncertainty and to open ourselves up to possible novelty.

Bigger-picture perception

The first model below shows two frames of reference, a personal square frame within an oval frame representing the context in which we currently operate. Our minds cannot cope with all of the information presented

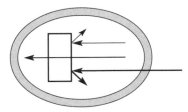

to us, so our perception is quite selective. In this simple model for thinking, three lines of information are presented as arrows. Familiar information, the central arrow, is recognized and perceived but the other two sources are quickly dismissed.

For most of us, as we age, our capacity to take in novelty reduces

The lower information stream could be significant because it arrives from outside the larger, outer context. This new information could be a rule-breaking opportunity or a threat because it arrives from a different context where different rules may apply. Novel information is often not seen as valuable simply because we lack the ability to perceive the opportunities it brings.

For most of us, as we age, our capacity to take in novelty reduces. As we become more experienced, our frames' increasing influence in favour of selective awareness reduces our ability to pay attention to new signals and original events, and therefore reduces also our ability to recognize original opportunities or risks. Consequently we can miss opportunities or completely overlook or wrongly interpret otherwise clear signals of impending threats. Such blind spots in our thinking process can be extremely dangerous for us as leaders. In our careers, a variety of blind spots in our thinking can limit our ability to progress.

The image of how we process our thoughts may be viewed as having two stages. We can allow our automated perception processes, symbol-

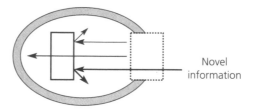

Novel
information

ized by the closed square, to dominate, or we can choose to employ a judgement-free style of thinking, as represented by the unformed square frame in second illustration. Easy to say, but actually quite hard to do.

So how can we flip these blinkers out of the way long enough to get some original thinking done? For a while try to:

- Stop convergent thinking.
- Stop demanding an answer.
- Stop analysis.
- Stop judging.
- Start divergent thinking.
- Be open.
- Play.
- Laugh.
- Be prepared to be surprised.
- Accept partial offers and interesting clues.
- Expect more interesting questions.

Feelings and thinking

Feelings at the edge

Our mobile, dynamic frames of reference are uniquely personal to each of us. They have both a logical and an emotional dimension. Inside the safe inner zone we can be logical and rational, comfortable, dry and humourless. Emotions are triggered when the boundaries of the frame are either crossed or disrupted. When a boundary is crossed over, there are two alternative reactions, namely laughter or anger. In each event the energy level rises.

In work situations, however, we may often feel constrained, even frustrated, by unwritten group behaviour rules that oblige us to contain our feelings. We tend to judge people if they fail to contain their feelings and, in doing so, reinforce some of life's unwritten rules.

Without passion, new ideas will lack zest and implementation will lack inspiration

Hemming in our feelings might be useful in some situations but is unhealthy when good-quality thinking is required. Without passion, new ideas will lack zest and implementation will lack inspiration. So if inspiration, high energy and great new ideas are what you want on a regular basis, then there needs to be a high tolerance for volatility of feelings. Creative tension is a normal feeling closely associated with a particular approach to productive thinking. It's normal, so don't bottle it – use it to power forward thought.

Hermit crabs and creative tension

When we dwell on a problem or an unrealized opportunity, we may feel dissatisfied or awkward. Some people will say they intuitively 'feel' there must be a better way, even though they do not fully understand what. Under these circumstances a real sense of tension builds up. We feel uncomfortable; we may feel irritated or hemmed in, even angry or frustrated. Creative tension will always involve the emotions.

In the preceding chapter I used a fighting crab as a picture tool to explain lopsided thinking. Now I'd like to employ an analogy of a hermit crab. Imagine yourself as such a creature, happy living in your borrowed shell, but as you grow bigger the shell becomes distinctly tight and uncom-

> **Tip** Ask yourself, how do I handle my emotions at work? Do I use my feelings well or do I control myself too much? Does this affect the quality of thinking and decision making? Consider how people in your organization behave. In your business search for brilliant new solutions alongside the pressure to succeed, how often do your colleagues get to laugh? If the answer is not often, then perhaps you are not using your full thinking potential and you are missing some practical fun! (For guidance on practical fun see Chapter 11.) If you are not laughing, you are unlikely to be learning, at the edge. If emotional expression is considered 'bad', then your organization will probably learn not to be creative.

fortable. Now your every living minute makes you aware you need a new, bigger shell to move into. The first difficulty is to locate a new shell. Then there will be the danger of being eaten by all your hungry neighbours as you make the move from the old to the unfamiliar new shell. Imagine the sense of relief when you finally arrive unscathed in your new home!

Back in the real world, imagine your frame of reference when you are trying to generate a solution to a subject so difficult you feel you are bulging under the pressure. Your 'frame' feels distinctly tight and uncomfortable and this is translated by your mind into a bodily sensation of real pressure. Then suddenly a solution, a really magnificent idea arrives, not quietly but BOOM! There's a rush of energy and happiness at having found the solution. The pressure is off and the tension eases. The energy level and positive attitude rise. There is a joy in resolution, in being released. This is just how the hermit crab must feel!

Changing shells will involve a degree of anxiety, followed by elation once we move into a bigger, more accommodating frame of reference. Let's be aware that emotion is involved in these thought processes. Often we will laugh. A new, bigger, more comfortable frame of reference is now in place. Laughter can be a sign of a problem in the process of being solved or a really big opportunity being realized.

When we employ divergent, creative thinking we may feel uncomfortable as we 'open up'. When we open up, mentally becoming more receptive, we immediately raise the mental energy level. Openness raises our tension levels. This tension is created by a lack of boundaries together with a sense of ambiguity. This is a state of creative tension. We should be aware of its presence and use the energy it delivers. Creative tension in groups can be great fun but occasionally, for individuals working alone over long periods, it can lead to feelings of isolation accompanied by a sensation of severe loss, an experience of 'an outpouring' because their boundaries are down. Creative people may appear to be overly emotional in the eyes of rational everyday types because of their creative 'exposure' to remaining open. Powerful creative types sometimes may need dull, repetitive situations in which to seek refuge. They also need extra latitude as regards rules, and 'reasonable' expectations from others, in order to deliver their best thinking.

> **Laughter can be a sign of a problem in the process of being solved or a really big opportunity being realized**

All of us can learn how to enjoy the feelings and sensations involved in being more creative. For more on creative thinking tools and behaviours, see Chapter 11.

In order to deal effectively with personal change, we need to be aware of and understand both individual and group frames of reference. It is difficult to energize anyone with a damaged frame of reference. If a person's or a group's frames of reference are robust yet reasonably flexible, then change may be more easily accommodated. All the notes in this book assume that intact, undamaged, healthy frames of reference are in place from the outset.

In summary

Frames of reference are both helpful *and* potentially harmful. They can speed up our decisions or trap us unwittingly. There are different ways of visualizing our frames of reference and how they overlap or interlink. Frames may be individual, multiple, communal and/or complex. Frames are 'alive'; they move and change. Many of the 'facts' that we believe make up our frames of reference may turn out to be assumptions or to be out of context or out of date. They need checking constantly. When we adjust, challenge or cross our frames of reference, feelings are always involved.

In coming to terms with our frames of reference, we need to retain enough structure to have useful habits. But we should regularly challenge our frames and our most basic assumptions in order to remain dynamic and open to new possibilities. We must retain a healthy degree of flexibility in the way we think, perceive and behave as adults if we are to remain viable in a rapidly changing world. By developing a higher level of awareness of the workings of different frames of reference, we are better placed to understand ourselves, other people and the reality we inhabit.

Interesting lives are never simple. Developing an appreciation of alternative points of view is a useful beginning to improving the way we think.

Now that we understand the two basic thinking directions and how frames work, we will look at how we might think about and cope with uncertainty, problems, ambiguity and context. The next chapters deal with these in turn.

What shapes my big picture | 4

Thinking is not something that happens in isolation. For example, when we think, our physiology can change and our behaviours may be modified. Thinking happens as part of a bigger pattern in which we play a role. The following notes are about some of the patterns I have witnessed or experienced.

Fixed patterns of perception

Some of our behaviours are embedded, habitual. That much is covered in Chapters 2 and 3. There is always a risk of becoming stereotyped, predictable and, yes, reliable, but boring too. Sometimes our patterns are good and sometimes bad for us.

Good driving habits keep us alive on busy highways. On the other hand we may be repeatedly attracted towards the wrong type of person who is not good for us, or the wrong kind of company, simply because we grew up in a particular industry or with a certain group of people. We may have unhealthy behaviour patterns towards exercise or food.

Behaviour and thinking are linked. All habits have a point of origin in thinking and learning. Habits can be recognized, mapped and in time redirected. But while physical or behavioural ones may be easy to detect, the thinking habits we have are much more difficult to spot.

I will now discuss some habitual thinking patterns. Once we are aware of these, we are in a better position to increase or decrease their impact on our thinking.

> **Tip** To detect fixed thinking patterns, look for frequent use of something you assume to be always and absolutely true. In some cases you may see a recurring experience. Look back through your experiences and attempt to find the common elements and ask why these were engaged or initiated. What are the assumptions attached to each component part of the repeating experience and to each player?

If you are *not* having fun with divergent thinking, then it probably isn't going to work well for you

Big patterns, small parts

In the search for our patterns, we might consider how our natural convergent and divergent thinking has patterns that determine the directions in which we think. Convergent thinking is often serious while the divergent variety is more fun. In fact if you are *not* having fun with divergent thinking, then it probably isn't going to work well for you. Knowing that laughter can be a sign of divergent thinking is a subtle part of an understanding that forms part of the pattern. The subtleties of patterns are important. For example, I can explain the logic of the two thinking pathways but, if I fail to point out the role of laughter, other people may not understand how to fully exploit their own creativity.

One, one, one

One of the most basic patterns of thinking is 'one-step' thinking, as well as the wrong assumption that speed is equal to quality. There seems to be a general assumption that faster, one-step conclusions are somehow better. Often people simply don't bother to follow through a line of possible extensions to the thought beyond the first step. Are we actually thinking when we use our minds in this particular way? I doubt it.

> **Tip** If you often feel an extrovert need to look important by responding fast, physically grip your tongue between your teeth and hold back your comments for a while – choose a better moment to offer your thoughts, when you have had a little more time to reflect. In that way other people will see that you have given the idea some thought. Then you can offer a more comprehensive response. People who react too quickly can sometimes be labelled as thoughtless.

Tip Young, ambitious people often associate decision-making authority with speed. This pattern is sometimes good, but not always so. Decisiveness is essential in a crisis but it is also easy to be fast and foolish (I know!). If you find yourself frequently coming up with quick, one-stop solutions, try to learn how to reflect. For example, you might employ this simple reasoning pattern to extend an idea:

'If x, then this may lead to y, so z, which leads to …'
– where x, y and z are different extensions of the idea or thought. Keep repeating this simple pattern until you arrive at new insights or conclusions.

Plodding and leaping

Many people seem to like to 'walk' their thinking in small, careful steps, where one clear step follows another. Others seem able to leap and bound ahead, missing several steps along the way. Whatever the explanation for this, the result is that the two types of people think and come to conclusions at very different speeds. The faster thinkers may actually be right in their conclusions, but they may not always be able (or willing) to spend time explaining themselves. It is also easy to imagine how the one type may irritate the other.

Tip If you are a rapid thinker, it may be easy to become irritated with someone who appears to you to be slower. Have patience. The other person may be just as intelligent as you are, but employ quite a different thinking pathway from you. If you are a thorough thinker who prefers one-step-in-front-of-the-other, 'thorough' patterns, try giving more freedom to those who 'leap around'; learn to trust them. Of course both types of thinker can make mistakes, but that is normal, so do not give up on the other once you start to collaborate.

One choice and only one choice?

One early lesson we adopt in the West is the clarity of right versus wrong. We seem to differentiate information by making use of extremes as boundaries. As a result, information may be clustered into patterns we can clearly recognize.

- Good and bad
- right and wrong
- either/or

are all examples of our inclination to polarize information for judgemental ends. Perhaps because of this, a frequent mistake people make in their thinking is to assume that their answers are exclusive of other answers. Usually time is wasted in competitive argument over which answer is correct. It is quite possible for two answers to be correct at the same time. Two different answers need *not* be mutually exclusive. Sometimes we need to unravel ideas from each other and see them as separate, independent and equally viable. Even contradictory concepts may co-exist in some situations.

> **Tip** Try replacing the phrase, 'Yes, but' with 'Yes, *and*'. It is not always necessary to stop and challenge. More than one option may be acceptable or desirable.

Staying out

If you want to imagine something, *stay out* of the frame for as long as you can stand it. I also observe that, when dealing with abstract ideas, people may often rush back towards rational thought when what is actually most beneficial is to stay with the more uncomfortable, often amusing ambiguity.

Moving between patterns

People sometimes adopt competitive postures in their thinking and will challenge the thinking and ideas of their colleagues in order to be seen to be in authority, in control. Other people like to demonstrate their incisive critical thinking ability and will pounce upon flaws and errors. Some like to sit in judgement. Then there are those that like to 'blue sky', to fly their thinking on a kite. All these thinking skills do have their place in business – that's why they are tolerated or encouraged.

To be effective in a fast-paced world, you must be able to move naturally and by choice through a variety of different thinking patterns. If you cannot adopt the different patterns, then you must be able to recognize them and be able to bring them out of people you work with.

Your favoured pattern will not always fit in with that of your colleagues, which is why when even highly intelligent people sit around a table for a meeting, the composite IQ can drop to shoe-size numbers. We rarely consider, 'What mode am I in now and is this mode of thinking appropriate now?'

Persistent patterns: Positional thinking

At a deeper level there are a number of basic innermost patterns and deeply ingrained drivers that affect the course of our thinking. The most obvious impact on thinking is the state of our health. That a healthy mind equals a healthy body remains good advice. If your emotions are rocked, then the course of your thinking will change and may become erratic. If you are challenged or threatened, then again the way you think may change too. These examples are obvious because they reflect extreme circumstances. Less obvious are the mundane everyday things that affect the way you think. Because these are less obvious, the impact they have on our thinking may be hidden from our conscious perception.

Where are you starting your thinking journey from? There are a variety of positions we adopt without realizing it that influence the course of our thinking. Next time you face a challenge, separate and listen to your own thoughts in motion. Get to know what happens in your own head. There are a variety of 'places and processes' that drive the quality of how we think, such as:

- time
- taped messages and other influences
- fixed patterns
- physiological influence
- availability.

Time: Thinking may be focused on the past, present or future

Imagine three people, one of whom seems to spend most of their time in the past, another in the future and the third in the present moment. (It is easy to imagine the first two, but perhaps a little more difficult to imagine the third, so here are a few examples of living in the present: a small child at play, an artist or a hedonist.) Consider what each of these people is like. What do their thinking patterns look like? What types of decisions do they take?

Each will have merits and demerits. No one place is perfect. We should all be able to move freely among the three places and be aware of the influences the past, the present and the future have upon us.

The past

If your thoughts are strongly influenced by the past (your own or someone else's), then you need to consider if these influences are worthy and useful to you now. Sometimes a past orientation is useful, sometimes not.

Changing the content of past influences on thinking is a matter of re-visualizing the memories once you have found something positive to focus on. We cannot change the past but we can re-package it and re-perceive it. Reconstruct the memory, the same events, but with different, positive focal points. Alternatively, if the old memory needs to be parked in neutral for later disposal, we can reframe the memories as substantially less important than they were by again thinking through new associations. Or learn simply to put the memory from your mind by focusing on the present (see 'Here and now', below).

> **We cannot change the past but we can re-package it and re-perceive it**

The future

The future is the classic Western, 'middle-class' mindset where people invest a lot of their present resources and energy in being concerned about what 'will' happen next. Often a belief will exist that we will be happier later when, for example, we retire, or pay off the mortgage or reach some other material target. An ability to think more clearly comes from accepting that you will do your best now and 'see' as a matter of blind faith what happens later, as it happens. If you do your best here and now, then there is nothing else to be done. Too much concern about the future blunts attention to what is happening now, in this present moment.

Tip People often expend vast amounts of concern and energy over future events or possibilities. I have found the idea of 'Punch Through' very helpful when faced with a seemingly overwhelmingly difficult task that is just over the horizon. The trick when faced with a perceived really big difficulty in the future is to prepare well and then to aim 'past' the future event. Then imagine being in the future looking back at having already achieved a good outcome. Focus on the desired outcome, not the barriers.

Here and now

Living 'in the moment' is a real gift to possess. Watch small children living like this and you can see why. Their thoughts during play are absolutely here and now. They are immediately open to surprise, to their imagination and to learning. As we age, we seem to drop this level of openness in favour of prediction and pleasure deferred. We worry more. One of the reasons why meditation and so many relaxation techniques work so well is they bring you into this very second, this infinite moment in time, into here and now. If all of your attention is on here and now, it is not possible to worry about the future or the past, which is where we expend much of our thinking energy. By learning to be 'here and now', we find that more energy is available and we find ease and clarity. When in the present moment we are open and can accept that something 'just is'; we need not explain it or deeply analyze it. In the present moment we can be aware of the presence of other things: we can acknowledge their presence but need not pay them attention. We simply exist in the moment. In this state of being we can experience heightened awareness, now.

> **Tip** Try yoga, meditation or anything your faith allows that will permit you to be totally relaxed and 'in the moment' for 15 minutes, three times a week, and you will see a marked improvement in your sense of well-being and in the clarity of your thinking.

Listening should be here and now. Generally speaking we are not very good at listening. Often the way we listen is to look for the opportunity to emphasize what we wish to say and to be recognized as taking part in the process.

> **Tip** Always try to hear the best in what is said. It is easy to make a listening mistake. For example, if you are feeling provoked by someone, politely ask the other person to restate what they said *and remain open*. You might say, 'I may have misheard something you just said. Please, would you tell me what you mean again but using different words?'

Old tapes can get in the way of moving forward; sometimes we need to rewind and re-record them

'Tapes'

Our frames of reference include experiences, images, lessons and a good number of 'tape recordings'. Some of these might have made perfect sense at one time, but may now be defunct. Old tapes can get in the way of moving forward; sometimes we need to rewind and re-record them. A simple example of an old tape that might be replayed is, when you sit down to dinner, 'You must always clean your plate' – that is to say, you *must* eat everything put in front of you. That message might have been good when you were a growing child but not now you are an adult, particularly if your body weight is too high.

> **Tip** Ask who the voice is on a recurring 'tape' message. Is it friendly? If not, try changing it. If the voice is hostile, change it to something silly such as a cartoon character – it's much easier to ignore then!

Where you are thinking from will shape *what* you think, your perceptions and many of your important lifestyle and business decisions. If your deep inner motivations are to do with being 'rich', being 'safe' or being a family person, or with experience of life or art, much of what you think will be processed in relation to these motivations. What you may hear during your thinking, as you rationalize a decision, is a particular message being played out in your mind that underscores why you believe your course of action is justified. You may even find that you use reinforcing statements in your conversations. For example, someone who frequently talks in terms of 'cut and thrust' may also talk about 'killing the opposition' and may deeply believe that 'life is a brutal fight'. The language you use, the messages you play back to yourself and the conversations with the people you associate with will all impact and reinforce your preferred patterns of thinking.

There are lots of more detailed books available on what motivates your thought processes and a variety of ways to access your deeper values. Suffice to say you should get to know your thought processes and the persistent messages you send yourself.

> **Tip** As the ancient Chinese proverb says, 'If you wish to conquer, first conquer yourself'. Get as many psychometric profiles on yourself as you can. Rarely will one method alone give you a true, dynamic picture of yourself, but several will give you some good pointers.

Physiological influences on thought

'Sticks and stones will break my bones but words will never hurt me' is a popular children's reply to taunts directed towards them. As a first line of emotional defence, this age-old response is not so bad, but it is not actually true: words can and do hurt. As a minimum, words and ideas affect our physiology and can subtly change us from moment to moment.

The brain does not differentiate between word pain and stick pain. Pain is pain. If the pain is abstract in nature, such as the pain inflicted by words, your mind will allocate the pain to a physical part of your body to make you aware you have pain. Pain has a purpose, namely to prevent damage by moving us away from something causing us injury. In this way, how we perceive what is said can impact the way we think.

Words do influence our physiology. Have someone talk slowly about fingernails scratching on a blackboard or talking about licking fresh-cut lemons and you will see a physical reaction. Words do alter our physiology, both negatively and positively. I have run an activity several times where the strength in someone's arm can be weakened by talking in a negative, dull way or strengthened by positive talk. These alterations take place subconsciously and have immediate effect. Other people's words will impact your thinking, your physiology and your sense of well-being.

Suffice to say, make sure you keep physically fit and that you stay mentally fit by 'swimming in clean, positive thoughts' and by keeping in the presence of good people. Avoid people and situations that are persistently negative.

Availability

One of the basic drivers of our thinking is our attitudes and beliefs about the availability or shortage of the things we think we need. This orientates us, like a compass needle, towards a particular direction. Our thinking and behaviour may contain quite a strong bias, for example life may be driven by a need to constantly be noticed, or to acquire money to avoid feeling

If we believe what we need is in short supply, we will fight all the harder to acquire or hoard it

insecure. A compelling drive to think and behave in a particular way may remain long after the need has been sufficiently met. If we believe what we need is in short supply, we will fight all the harder to acquire or hoard it.

The things we need may not always be material, but could also be time, attention or something else that is equally useful. Intangible, fundamental need orientation could include attention, affection, advice, hugs, information, direction or any number of other similar gestures.

Our orientation, though, need not be automatic: it can be considered as a choice and therefore adjustable. With sustained effort we can reassess and redirect our thoughts and behaviours.

Look at this checklist:

- So, what is scarce?
- Is it truly unavailable or rare?
- Is it still important and if so why?
- Is it the only choice and if so why?
- What alternatives are available?
- What other positive options or choices are there?
- What is available in big quantities now?
- We sometimes forget the little things. What have you overlooked recently?
- How does this impact the way you think?
- Does your current orientation help you or hinder you?

This sort of checklist works just as well for considering how your business or product might be repositioned.

In summary

Your thinking can be affected either by fixed patterns – whether you are naturally a one-step thinker, a leaper or a plodder, or whether you believe there is only ever one right answer – and by where you start your thinking from. Positional thinking is a broad term I use to consider the places from which you begin thinking journeys. Wherever you begin, be it from a position in time or from a deep personal need or from a particular view on the 'availability' of what you need, your thinking may be significantly predisposed. In turn, if you always have just the one destination in mind for your journey, then that too will impact the way the world is perceived.

It is worth considering 'Where am I coming from?' before you engage a serious thought process, to see if your own thinking is likely to work in a complementary or detrimental way.

This chapter has looked at positions we adopt before we begin our thinking. One of the important factors shaping the way we think is how we deal with certainty and the sense of risk as well as associated sensations of excitement and fear. When we think about any major issue, we must consider the degrees of certainty and uncertainty.

Our perception of certainty has an impact on how we live our lives from day to day as well as the way we think and react to new situations and to problems. In other words, the quality of our thought processes will change depending upon how secure or how certain we feel. Before we engage our thinking about an uncertain situation, the first checkpoint should be our personal sense of safety and certainty. Once we have attained some internal sense of security we may then be better able to think more clearly about an uncertain external situation. The next chapter looks at certainty, uncertainty and risk in more depth.

Finding clarity and certainty | 5

Contexts. Our ability to cope with uncertainty and its effect on thinking

One of the key factors in shaping an attitude to openness is how we individually perceive 'certainty'. A sense of who we are and what we stand for is essential to our mental health. We all need anchor points of some sort to help us retain a grip on reality. If our sense of certainty is undermined, the way we think shifts. In order to be able to work smarter rather than harder as a reflex reaction to change, we need to understand and manage our perceptions about certainty.

We each of us need a sense of certainty, but the amount we need may vary considerably from person to person and from time to time. Also the nature of what we need to know as 'certain' will vary. Therefore certainty is a personal issue. What one person sees as certain is unlikely to be the same as another. We may share some common ground in this area with other people, but our personal pattern of certainties taken as a whole will be uniquely ours. Even in things we regard as tangible or as matters of fact, we cannot be absolutely certain they will remain true or certain over time. For example, our views on the nature of work or the laws of science may prove not to be true in the future.

Certainty need not be based on something tangible; for example a sense of certainty could be based upon a sense of faith or a set of values. On a philosophical note, we may well discover that intangible certainties such as our beliefs or values are the more durable certainties over time.

A sense of certainty relates to how confident we are about here and now and about events in the future. Our sense of certainty and uncertainty is shaped in several different ways.

First, let's consider our capacity to hold information and model it into predictions. One way we humans adopt a sense of certainty is to hold enough information to make short-term predictions about what might happen next. As a species, our minds are particularly good at making use of patterns and extrapolating predictions. If information striking our senses fails to fit a pattern, we have the choice to either dismiss it or explore it. We can rehearse in our minds how a series of events might play out under different circumstances. We rehearse the future possibilities, the interactions and the outcomes. Sometimes we do this for fun – we indulge in a little fantasy or daydream or we indulge our imagination in a good 'whodunnit' film. At other times this activity may be essential to survival: a soldier may have to predict what his enemy may do next. In daily life we may try to anticipate a conversation so we can be ready to respond. We all have varying degrees of this predictive capacity.

A second dimension will have something to do with the time needed to feel confident in reacting to new information. Some people can run faster than others. Some are sprinters, others are long-distance marathon devotees while others still prefer a slow stroll. One person may have enough predictive ability and imagination to quickly grasp the impact of novel information, using the bare minimum of input to reach a sense of 'certainty'. In contrast, someone else may take forever processing the same information to arrive at a useful conclusion. If you asked people with different information-processing needs what would constitute an early decision, quite different answers would be produced.

> **Tip** Do not assume that your thinking speed is normal and that other people 'should' think at your speed. Fast and slow thinking each have their own advantages and disadvantages.

Our ability to develop a sense of certainty depends upon the confidence we have in ourselves and our relationship with the 'world' we occupy. Your world will be very different from mine and from everyone else's because each person's frames of reference are unique. In addition, our sense of certainty requires us to judge the reliability we attach to new information and its context. If all information is known, nothing can surprise us. Nothing will be novel. Nothing will shock us. We might feel secure but bored.

It is important we give conscious thought to our attitude to risk and certainty because in some, risk is a source of excitement, while in others it is a cause for distress. The way we use our minds when we are distressed will differ from when we are not. So at what point do we regard something as risky?

If we are familiar with something, we possess awareness of what generally is expected to happen next. Awareness of, and confidence in, one's future can reduce the stress of uncertainty. If we have prior positive experience of a similar situation, this also reduces the stress (or excitement) of uncertainty. A joke is never as funny the second time around. An exciting experience eventually becomes known and then ordinary. When we have a well-formed frame of reference for a subject that we know and understand very well, it might become boring. When this happens there is no novelty, no sense of danger or risk and no potential for surprise. By contrast, if we reflect on what we have found exciting, we find high shock value, i.e. high novelty. In other words, the unfamiliar holds the potential to shock and thereby either excite or worry us. The degree to which we will seek out or avoid risk is therefore a matter of how we cope with stress and how we view our own sense of certainty.

Tip The danger of familiarity is complacent thinking. If something warrants your alert attention, try to refresh your view of it by changing any established habits towards it.
Approach it in a different way; try adding new dimensions. Ask someone really young for their opinion on it.

Most people have survived a bungee jump without injury. There are those who go for a bungee jump trusting they will survive, whereas there are people (like me!) who imagine damage to their eyes, brains, spines and general sense of well-being and refuse to play. What some people take as a thrill-maker makes others feel uncertain and at high personal risk. So in developing a model for thinking about risk, we should include the sense of certainty in the same model since the level of risk and the level of certainty seem to be linked:

- High sense of certainty equals low novelty, low surprise
  - low risk and low emotional content.
- Low sense of certainty equals high novelty, high surprise
  - high risk and high emotional content.

How much risk we take is perhaps proportional to how certain we feel about likely outcomes. Risk is more likely to be influenced by feeling than by logic because risky behaviour pushes against the boundaries of our frame of reference and can trigger deep self-preservation instincts.

Tip Generally, in business, 'feelings' take second place to logic and are seen to be detrimental rather than useful. However, when dealing with uncertainties, feelings can be an instinctive, useful guide to decision making. Try to harness your awareness of the presence of such feelings. Be aware of how and where your body reacts and try to decipher the message. The message your body sends you will be crude. The intuition may be a simple yes/no/avoid/wrong!/trust/do not trust/strange/go for it/leave now! Try to remember your instinctive decision if you choose to use a rational thought process. Review the decision later to see if instinct would have given a better or worse result. Look at the circumstances: where and when do instincts produce a better result for you?

Steve Carter, a founding partner of Apter International Ltd, has a useful model to help people think about uncertainty. He refers to 'the dangerous edge' and describes a mountaineer standing by a steep precipice. Beyond the dangerous edge is a trauma zone. The confidence the mountaineer has is based upon experience, skill and trust in the equipment and his or her colleagues. Despite the presence of clear danger, the mountaineer operates with a sense of certainty and feels safe and confident that he or she can stay out of the trauma zone.

Working from the comfort zone towards the edge of an existing frame of reference, where there are unknown possibilities, is where new learning takes place. By working at the edge we can learn and extend the frame of reference into a bigger one by encompassing new experiences. Our sense of certainty is something that can be proactively modified through learning.

A certainty tool: The time-line funnel

Earlier we looked at our ability to feel confident if we can safely predict something. Prediction involves the ability to see, understand, remember and rehearse patterns of events. One of the basic dangers in thinking about a future event is that we may fail to consider the effect that the movement of time will have upon the probability of something happening the way we expect. There is the danger that we will take 'static' snapshots of reality and assume that these will remain true. Over time we can be less certain about what we currently regard as true. The

The further out in time we look, the more uncertainty we are faced with

further out in time we look, the more uncertainty we are faced with. As certainty decreases, the possibility for risk increases.

One way of dealing with this is to use the following 'time-line funnel' tool for thinking about the broad concepts of certainty and risk. If we can visualize a pattern, we can employ it to think about a variety of certain and uncertain business situations such as strategy and innovation. The time-line funnel tool may also help us to map out and manage certain types of 'open problems'.

Certainty

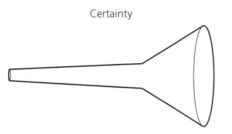

A time-line funnel is a very simple shape that we can employ to think about the relationship between certainty and future risk. The inside of the funnel represents the predictable boundaries we operate within over time. Use the image by assuming most of us work and think inside the narrow rational boundaries defined by the narrow spout of the funnel. When we look further forward in time, our sense of certainty moves from the spout to the mouth. The size of the inside of the time-line funnel at the beginning suggests that the range of variation or risk is relatively low and relatively well known for the short term. As we look further forward in time, the boundaries of what can be regarded as certain begin to widen. So, the relatively well-known, predictable boundaries are in the narrow spout while the wide area of uncertainty or risk is represented by the wide mouth of the funnel.

Of course there are many shapes of spouts and time-line funnels, each representing different patterns of certainty and uncertainty.

A simple example of a short time-line funnel model would be northern European weather forecasting. A reasonable degree of accuracy in the forecast, say plus or minus 15 per cent, is sufficient for the user to confidently predict the likely weather in the next three days. Beyond that the odds widen and after a week or two the weather predictions cannot be relied upon beyond 'the sun tends to shine in summer and sometimes we have snow in winter'. Clearly the latter forecast is useless to a big retailer whose sales may be affected by weather, especially if they operate in England where we sometimes get all four of nature's seasons in one week!

Our personal ability to forecast future events may be a question of how much we are prepared to tolerate uncertainty and the type and context of the decision arena. For example, the rates of technological change are much slower in the construction industry than for microchip technologies.

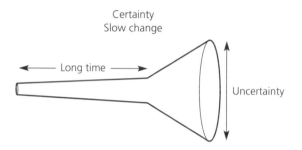

When variation is known, we can plan and prepare rationally. The thin end of the time-line funnel is where we can employ rational planning and lots of lovely logic and analysis. People who prefer to 'live' within a narrowly bounded and predictable view of the world will think and behave in a way that will reflect their bounded perspective. They will want to be able to consider the future as measurable, quantifiable and quite predictable. In a position of authority, such people might expect their employees to provide specific detailed facts and schedules about the future. This is realistic if the long term is likely to remain the same and if no major discontinuities occur. But in some business arenas, such as the disk drive and microchip industries, planning as little as 18 months ahead or even less may be considered long range.

Hard data, defined schedules and firm conclusions are of limited value in rapidly changing environments

The time-line funnel model's utility as a thinking tool lies in its revelation that there is more to planning than thinking rationally. Hard data, defined schedules and firm conclusions are of limited value in rapidly changing environments because of the existence of huge potential for future variation or risk. Being capable of thinking about open-ended issues is increasingly becoming a prerequisite skill for people

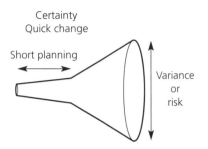

Certainty
Quick change

Short planning

Variance
or
risk

dealing with rapid change. Anyone who aspires to be the guardian of an organization, a change agent, a politician or a senior executive needs to be able to think and operate in the wider end of the funnel.

The time-line funnel model also helps us to consider the nature and impact of human diversity and tolerance. Assuming people are free to choose their working or living environments, different people are likely to choose situations that reflect their inclinations and thinking preferences. The time-line funnel model suggests at least three major mindsets or lifestyle preferences that could be applied in situations both in and outside of work.

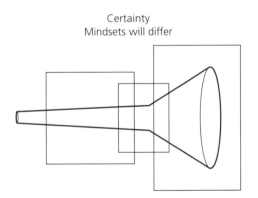

Certainty
Mindsets will differ

The squares overlaid represent people's three different frames of reference with regard to assumptions about 'reality'. Thus the time-line funnel model might help to explain different attitudes towards a variety of degrees of risk within organizations. In reality, more than one frame of reference is necessary to run a business effectively in the long term; however, each has a different role. Each frame will have quite different boundaries beyond which they cease to add value. Each person's frame will define and express what they strongly believe to be good reasons for having their reasonable limits. For example, compare and contrast the lifestyle, aspirations and behaviours of someone who occupies the frame on the right with someone from the left frame. Would they generally:

- be relatively dull or relatively exciting
- be conventionally reliable or conventionally unreliable
- be predictable or unpredictable
- enjoy detail or dislike detail
- enjoy big surprises or dislike big surprises
- dislike and resist change or provoke change?

We can see how people with different frames of reference, as depicted in this model, might clash or complement each other depending upon how well each understands the deeper needs and contribution of their colleagues.

The time-line funnel model can also help us to unravel 'wide-open' or ill-defined questions. For example, I recently attended a rather frustrating workshop on 'knowledge management'. Usually my frustration is a strong indication that I need to learn something quite big (other than patience). The workshop was discussing the question 'What is knowledge management?' The most fundamental piece of original insight to be offered as an answer was that asking about knowledge management is to ask a very broad question indeed. I was frustrated to repeatedly hear answers that seemed to me to be very wide of the mark. However, once I understood that the fault lay in the primary question, 'What is knowledge management?', I had a map I could use, namely the time-line funnel. Using the time-line funnel to illustrate my thinking, I applied the same question across the length of the funnel and the frames of reference that accompany the three major zones. For example, to a highly task-oriented person at the narrow end of the funnel, knowledge management might mean knowing where to get the best deal on A4 paper supplies. This would be their functional 'reality' of knowledge management. Contrast that mindset with that of a board director making billion-dollar strategy decisions from the wide end of the time-line funnel. Knowledge management under these conditions might mean high-value decision support. In between these two extremes there might be all sorts of variations of opinion on what actually constituted knowledge management. As an ill-defined term, 'knowledge management' is clearly going to be much too broad to have any real value within a big organization. Knowledge management could mean too many different things to too many different people in the same organization, resulting in a high potential for confusion and misallocation of time and resources. The solution would be to use other, more specific terms that meant something to the organization at different levels.

In all probability the volume of information flows will, over time, become problematic and what will be more valuable will be the activities that maximize flows of timely wisdom. Because the term knowledge management is already devalued by its diverse meanings, new definitions will need to be created about precisely what is needed by whom and why it will add value. There will most likely be multiple tactical, strategic systems, processes and behaviours.

Anything that has an impact on wisdom flows will have to remain sufficiently dynamic to allow forward evolution

The time-line funnel model would suggest that anything that has an impact on wisdom flows will have to remain sufficiently dynamic to allow forward evolution.

Thus, if you were given the task of addressing an ill-defined problem labelled with a meaningless title, the time-line funnel model might help you to think about the character of the problem from multiple perspectives.

To get into the time-line funnel pattern of thinking, there are two options:

- Use the time-line funnel to think about the three major frames of reference.
- Use it to place the issue in three or more points in time with different constraints.

To focus on the three frames of perspective, simply think about the issue from each frame along the time-line funnel:

- The narrow area of the funnel, where everything is relatively well defined and focused task activities predominate. The main concerns here are about definition, fit, documented process, rules, reproducible quality, compliance and here-and-now issues.
- The wide area of the funnel, where issues tend to be bigger, long term and ill defined. The main concerns here are about exploring, finding strange new things, strategy, vision, relative positioning, developing unique advantages, opening up new options for the future and future needs.

- The middle area of the funnel. In between the two extremes the issues are about the linkages between the present and the future. Interests here might include gregarious networking, sharing problem solving, crafting from raw material and developing but not running – people are unlikely to be 'completer-finishers'.

To use the time-line funnel from a time perspective, then think about how the person or the issue would sit when

- highly defined, restricted and confined in the narrow zone of the present
- very loosely defined, virtually unrestricted and in no way confined in the wide-open zone of the long term
- at the intermediate point of the medium term with some definition and some freedoms.

Scenarios

Utilizing the time-line funnel approach can help us in our thinking about how we face the future. We can easily 'see' that there will be at least two types of thinking about planning for the future. One is an art, the other a science; one rational, the other creative. In addition, we can see that different types of people might contribute from quite different perspectives.

When leaders are faced with a wide range of uncertainties or high volatility, they need to be able to develop planning as an 'art' form. A logical, numeric, scientific approach will not work where logic does not yet exist. The wide mouth of the funnel suggests that variation is high, that constraints and boundaries that would otherwise provide clear points of reference do not yet exist as they do in the bounded area of the narrow spout.

Scenarios can be used to make sense of complex, unformed futures by making explicit a variety of risks and opportunities that would otherwise tend to remain hidden until too late. Scenarios work by bringing together future uncertainties in clusters. Once major forces are set relative to each other, a form of reasoning and intelligent debate can emerge. In scenarios the reasoning produces distinctly separate 'future worlds'. Usually a few scenario models will turn out to be useful in helping you build a small number of bridges between the present and these future worlds.

Having produced an image of possible futures that you and your colleagues can agree on, it now becomes possible to do both formal planning and creative planning. Once created, formalized scenarios present a range of possibilities that can encourage you to stay alert for alternative outcomes and pay attention to the possibility of alternative futures. Good scenarios stop us from assuming the future will be a minor variation of today. Scenario planning can be an excellent tool for stretching your thinking ability about the uncertainty of the future.

Good scenarios stop us from assuming the future will be a minor variation of today

There are a variety of approaches to scenario planning. Because of the wide range of possibilities regarding the future, there is a risk of drowning busy managers in heaps of boring irrelevant data, especially if the scenario-planning process is led by detail-oriented types. When handled well, scenario planning promotes intellectual dexterity in a wide group of people and can create a common language for a wider discussion among more employees about the future. Management insight about possible futures using the collective intelligence of the organization can then be worked up to produce contingent plans and hard numbers.

Tip Explore a variety of scenario-planning approaches, of which there are several.

Tip Creative thinking skills are a credible way of alerting the mind to a volatile future in both one's personal and work life.

Betting

Using a time-line funnel model does not guarantee any particular outcome, though. The funnel shape simply shows the existence of a range of possibilities across the timescale and the boundaries of probability. To a large degree, the ability to forecast into the widening funnel requires both broad vision and, in the absence of a magic crystal ball, the ability to place bets, to gamble. If you wait for information to condense, more people will recognize the value and you may lose first-mover advantage. On the other hand, in moving too early you may be plain wrong. So it's a bet. In betting, success and failure will depend upon the odds and the investment.

In any event no one ever wins *all* the time, so you will need to be OK with error and be resilient enough to learn and move on quickly. Error is normal. In fact if you are not making mistakes, you are probably not making progress. If you somehow create an environment in which mistakes are considered bad, then your wider decision systems will be compromised. The way you think about error is very important: see Chapter 7.

Most of us like to live in a rational world and we would like to think that someone somewhere has a plan into which our lives can be placed in an orderly fashion. Perhaps many of us would not regard gambling and betting as credible management skills, but that would be a rational view and a partial truth – is betting not the same as risk taking? Betting is not necessary in situations where most or all of the facts are known; logical extrapolation and scientific deduction will suffice in well-defined realities as in the narrow spout of the timeline funnel. As certainty reduces and action is required to precipitate a result, betting on incomplete information becomes increasingly necessary in fast-changing environments. Inventors and entrepreneurs will progress an idea or attempt to pioneer novel products to as yet non-existent markets based on a bet and faith in their own instincts.

> **If you are to capitalize on a bet on the future, you will also need the ability to follow through and implement quickly**

Those who are betting on information from the wide-open funnel will often face greater risk than those who focus on the spout, but competitive pressure is likely to be less and the rewards of success disproportionately high for the early entrants to new markets or processes. Success is not guaranteed, though: if you are to capitalize on a bet on the future, you will also need the ability to follow through and implement quickly.

Naturally, reducing risk is important but spreading several bets is just as important. We should try to prepare for different eventualities and, where possible, to stack the odds in our favour through contingency planning and preparation. Early preparatory moves are often relatively low cost in terms of time, money and resources. However, most of us tend to have to work with finite resources, so it is not possible to cover *all* bets. In the end, the longer game is a gamble.

Are you a master of tasks, a weaver or a dreamer?

We tend to think and behave according to personal preferences. Each of us possesses a wide range of abilities, but we tend to use only familiar thinking patterns that work. We will eventually settle down at the position along the funnel where we feel most comfortable. Some people love detail and certainty while others prefer 'wide-open' thinking. In order to cover the range of thinking required to consider the future, there are at least two options open to us. We either teach most of the leadership and senior management people how to think in different ways and to codify when each thinking style is relevant, or we use highly rational people for narrowly defined types of task and far-horizon thinkers for long-range planning. In between the two we use what I call 'weavers'. These are people who are comfortable as go-betweens and can translate dreams and the intangibles into processes that the task types can cope with. In order for this to work and to be sustainable, each person needs explicit recognition for their contribution from the other types.

> **Tip** Assess where your own thinking preferences place you within the funnel model and team up with two other people who occupy two quite different frames of reference.

> **Tip** If you are working in the wide-open, high-uncertainty area, interesting questions are important. If you are operating in the narrower well-defined mouth of the funnel, having the right answers becomes most important. Ask yourself 'Am I in possession of some interesting questions about the future?' If the answer is no, then you may have a blind spot or two as regards your future.

Strategic leadership competencies

The time-line funnel model shows us that different thinking skills are needed according to the volatility of the environment. It also shows us that change is inevitable as time passes. Ultimately organizations will require strategic direction to deal with future uncertainty. The ability to think within the wider funnel is vital if you intend to lead other people in the long term.

As people are given increasing responsibility for the effective running of major projects or organizations, the ability to think strategically will be essential for their long-term viability. The skills required where the funnel is wider, that is to say in highly uncertain conditions, will include:

The ability to think within the wider funnel is vital if you intend to lead other people in the long term

- a higher tolerance of uncertainty
- an ability to remain 'open'
- the ability to cope with partial information
- the ability to screen and select valuable gems hidden within large amounts of information
- the ability to resolve conflicts in information
- the ability to deal with ambiguity
- being fast enough to extrapolate from an emerging pattern
- the ability to quickly assess a variety of consequences of a pattern
- the ability to place bets with only partial information
- the ability to reassure other people who need certainty
- social skills
- networking skills
- oratory skills
- mass communication and influencing skills.

Most experienced managers will recognize the list, but how many can say they have had formal tuition in any or all of the above? A few of these skills are honed during business training simulations and others might be gained through direct experience.

> **Tip** One of the best ways to make tacit skills explicit is to set yourself the task of teaching them. If you were to teach a younger colleague about how to think about and deal with the non-rational aspects of business life, where would you start and what methods would you use? Once you have worked this out, you can pass on the skills and in doing so you will enhance your own abilities.

Planning time

Two additional issues are noteworthy concerning the funnel model. The first is that people and organizations must determine for themselves how far ahead they can predictably plan and at what point it becomes futile because of the range of variables. At that point, drop the pen and pick up the brush: the planning from now on is an art form!

The fact that many Western organizations adopt a five-year timespan for their strategic plans seems to me to be highly illogical, given that the forces acting upon their individual situations will be vastly different. Even if an organization was once, many years ago, correct in adopting five years as the outer limit for planning, why should that remain true today?

Tip It is likely that the shape of the time/certainty funnel will shorten in many industries as overall industry reaction times accelerate. Check the pace of change in your industry and consider changing the way you plan. Adopt a smarter way for plotting horizons.

In summary

Over time, frames of reference cannot always be relied upon to remain true to their original form. Building upon the previous chapter, we have seen that frames of reference can move towards or away from each other over time. As time passes, we cannot be sure of what might happen and predicting what will happen next becomes increasingly problematic.

Experience suggests that in business and biology we can also expect that completely new frames of reference will evolve in the future. The funnel model can help us to see that there are limits to rational thought processes when it comes to predicting the future. Leaders who are required to deal with uncertain conditions require skills in 'open' creative thinking together with an ability to deal with and place bets based upon incomplete information. With this in mind, the next three chapters look at how we might think about problems, error and ambiguity.

Working it out

6

In previous chapters we looked at the basic direction our thoughts could take and we examined models of the lenses through which we view the world, our frames of reference. This chapter is intended to help us think about problems and choice.

In a state of pure innocence there are no choices.

The moment we have to make a choice we must make judgements. Some are simple but many are not. Our ability to make choices depends to some extent on how we view risk and certainty. I hope to show in this chapter how problems might be visualized to help us think about our choices.

Thinking about problems begins with the word itself. Eskimos have many different words for snow that quickly characterize local conditions. We in the West have a limited choice of words for problems. The Japanese, on the other hand, have different descriptions for problems; there are those that produce a benefit and those that do not. In the Western paradigm problems are mostly viewed negatively. The word paradigm is used here to describe a holistic pattern of rules, beliefs and behaviours that a group of people work within – a bigger group frame of reference if you like. An alternative view would be to regard problems as a learning opportunity, an introduction to a new path or a blessing. Problems can create a sense of purpose, which generates a sense of personal relevance. Many people relish the idea of a problem-free life. However, when we have no problems at all, we risk losing a sense of purpose and may cease to feel relevant; we risk becoming pointless. Imagine a world with absolutely no challenges, a life of total ease; for a while it would be pleasant but eventually life would be unexciting and dull. Sometimes very successful people or very wealthy individuals can experience severe difficulty with their lives because everything is too easy. There is no stretch, no learning, no point. The nature of the problems we choose to adopt can sometimes define who we are.

> **Tip** We could choose to change the way we think about our difficulties and say 'Problems are great! Thank goodness for problems!'

In the absence of problems, would we exist in a state of bliss or eternal numbness?

Without problems sales people would have nothing to offer. In the absence of problems, would we exist in a state of bliss or eternal numbness? How would we know the difference? Problems may cause discomfort, but some are healthy and provide useful stimuli to stretch our abilities. It is not unusual, therefore, to find people looking for or creating problems.

Types of problem

In many cases people will try to resolve a problem in order to remove the sense of discomfort. They may resolve their discomfort by avoiding or transferring the problem, or by attempting some form of fix. In attempting to resolve a problem, few people give consideration to the type of problem they are dealing with before they choose a course of action.

There are basically two types of problem. Type 1 is characterized as one where a solution can be 100 per cent realized and the outcome can therefore be maximized. In Type 1 problems, the more you study to uncover the relevant facts, the closer you will come to an absolutely correct answer. One might refer to this type of problem as being 'maximal' or 'clear cut'.

The nature of the second type of problem is that it is not at all clear cut: it is 'slippery'. This second type of problem lacks clarity because it is subject to different interpretations by different people. With a 'slippery' problem someone will usually disagree with a solution that meets the needs of others. 'Slippery' problems are characterized as having solutions that can only ever be *optimized* and a full, clear-cut resolution is never possible. This second problem type can only be resolved by compromise.

Notice that the nature of problems has been defined by their *likely outcome*. This is important because people often make the mistake of charging straight at a problem as if they are *all* clear cut and 100 per cent resolvable, without first considering the most likely outcome.

In both cases failure or success is possible, but only with the clear-cut type can an absolutely perfect answer be found. With slippery problems, no matter how hard one works, there will never be an absolutely right answer. The benefit of acknowledging the difference between the two types is we can save wasted effort and heartache on the slippery ones.

Let's look at some examples to show the nature of the two problems. A typical example of a clear-cut problem would be to discover the fastest way to travel between two fixed locations, for example from your home town to the capital city. More time and study will lead to a better-quality answer until eventually a perfect route is found. By contrast, an example of a slippery problem would be to ask a group of people to determine what would be the best form of education.

Study and research can logically resolve the first and there will be an absolutely correct answer. The second is a matter of opinion and no matter who is asked, views will vary as to what comprises 'best' or what constitutes 'education'. Even if you discover a really good education system you always leave someone disadvantaged. Clearly the two types of problem need to be dealt with differently.

Even if you discover a really good education system you always leave someone disadvantaged

Regrettably, naive managers sometimes assume that all problems are the same and that their role is to solve all problems by driving other people to come up with clear-cut, detailed answers. As the pressure for performance rises within results-biased organizations, the temptation to act first and think later may lead to less effective work and increased anxiety, especially if people fail to think about the type of problem and assume that all are clear cut. In fact while some management problems are indeed clear cut in nature, they are in the minority.

As we can see from the example above, a lack of awareness of the nature of problems can lead to some pretty unhealthy behaviour. Attempts to find the right answer result in what I call the search for 'the spreadsheet for everything'. The assumption is that the correct answer is simply a matter of collecting all the variables and mapping them on to a huge computerized mathematical spreadsheet! When another fact turns up to confound the process, it gets added to the spreadsheet. As the spreadsheet grows ever bigger and bigger to accommodate more and more variables, the clear-cut answer remains just as unattainable as it ever was.

The approach to problem solving must be aligned with the basic structure of the problem.

Illustrating the point

If the problem is essentially optimal or slippery, then no amount of study will ever allow all variables to be neatly accommodated in either the correct or incorrect camp. Slippery problems always involve compromise and a degree of 'fuzziness'. To illustrate this I will use a series of different simple images.

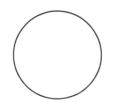

The world simply 'is'.

The first shape is a simple circle that represents a world of information. The world simply 'is'. There is no right. There is no wrong. For the sake of this illustration, let's say that everything within conscious awareness lies within the circle. There has been no differentiation between things, and all thoughts are without judgement or place or time. There is no relativity.

When we choose to make a decision, we attempt to classify good and bad or right and wrong information, or we try to separate useful from not useful. This is represented in its simple form in the diagram below.

Information is judged

*The information falls into clearly
defined, absolute areas.*

We can use this simple shape to represent the first kind of problem, that where clear-cut results can be achieved. In order for us to find a clear answer, the information must be divisible into correct or incorrect. If we were to divide this particular 'world' with a line, the line would fall with 100 per cent of the correct information on one side.

Some people understand the nature of problems and are even prepared to forgive politicians

If we can insert such a line with complete certainty, we know the decision to be a clear on/off or right/wrong one. The decision can be maximized; 100 per cent efficiency can be achieved. So far, so good, but unfortunately this type of problem is not so common. Tacitly, we know that the world of decision making is not quite as simple as suggested by the pure decisions illustrated above.

Some people understand the nature of problems and are even prepared to forgive politicians – some of the time! If you dislike political thinking, then perhaps you may not understand the nature of the decisions politicians often face. Whether you are an everyday member of a team or a senior manager, a parent or a lover, ultimately you will be faced with some level of political complexity. The question is, how will you do well for yourself? Consider the following series of images as simple maps of the nature of complex decisions.

Slippery problems

Try to draw a straight line through the diagram below. Your goal is to get as much of one of the colours on one side of the line as possible. What do you see? How would you interpret what you see if you had to make a decision based on information that shaped up like this? Also, what do the smaller circles suggest? What might they represent?

Yin and Yang

This Yin and Yang representation of the real world is very useful. If information or people fall into the different domains in this particular holistic view, then you may 'see' more clearly what your options are. This diagram shows one option you might have taken with a complex problem.

If the next picture represented, for example, a pay bonus scheme in a large company and the line divided the group to be rewarded from the

group to be excluded, how would you expect people to feel? On balance would you have a good or a bad decision? Compare this with the diagram below where the dividing line is in a different position.

The complexity of most of life's problems is neatly shown in the two diagrams above. A divided Yin–Yang image helps us to think about several aspects of complicated, slippery problems. If we assume that the dark-coloured domain is what we wish to include then, no matter how we divide it up with our line of decision, people will be left out who should be still in, while other people will be included who clearly ought to be left out! Furthermore there will be a glaring self-contained issue in the middle of the domain that gets left isolated and unresolved (see the two smaller circles). Decisions about bonus schemes and the sharing of resources often end up looking like this.

In the illustration below, I have added arrows to the line that cuts the decision in order to suggest a few degrees of freedom within which optimized results can still be obtained.

Optimize, but decide quickly

In other words, once an optimal response to this kind of problem has been devised, some people or issues will be wrongly excluded. Whichever way the decision is adjusted, the overall result remains a compromise. People who demand a 100 per cent answer to or resolution of a complex subject will eventually accuse the decision maker of fudging the issue. In so doing, the accuser will demonstrate their lack of understanding and their intellectual inflexibility.

People who have to make choices within complex situations can never please everyone all the time

> **Tip** When thinking about slippery problems, start from the perspective of the supplementary problems that will be created by the various solutions. Which solution will minimize disenfranchisement? This is not always easy to tease out, but it is necessary if you want to arrive at a productive compromise.

Politicians and people who have to make choices within complex situations can never please everyone all the time. The sliced Yin–Yang models above illustrate this dilemma quite nicely.

When we are able to understand the essential differences between slippery and clear-cut problems, we can save time by agreeing with others the nature of the issues, the possible choices, the type of problem and the context in which these operate *before* we offer our response.

A simple but not uncommon example of a clear-cut expectation wrongly applied to a 'slippery' problem is the senior manager who demands a highly detailed, long-term strategic forecast with a complete detailed analysis of all future risks and opportunities. This is a sure recipe for frustration.

> **Tip** Outside of a true crisis, when faced with a request for significant action, ask for time to consider the question, even if it is only a few minutes. Always think first about the nature of the question and ask for clarification of the expected result before agreeing to comply. Challenging the request at this stage saves wasted effort later, especially if the request and the expected result are mismatched.

More complex still: Yin and Yang rotate!

My picture that best gives shape to slippery problems has another twist to it. The picture should not be thought of as static in time.

In other words, to choose an optimum decision and fix it down in the rulebook would be wrong because the whole shape can rotate or wobble or rock! So the decision-making process has to be alert to changes and equally flexible in order to constantly optimize for the best outcome. What is right now may soon be wrong. Decisions involving slippery problems are only ever temporary compromises. As conditions change and the system rotates, the same decision looks progressively different.

Context and problems

Decisions are rarely made in isolation and are usually made within some form of context. The context may include a place, a relevant situation, other people and/or an environment. Sometimes the context in which a problem sits may be complex and there may be areas of subtle but disproportionate influence. Rushing into a decision or acting without reflecting on wider issues may produce unexpected consequences.

On occasion the attempt to resolve one problem leads to the evolution of several more problems of a greater magnitude. Sometimes the best response is no response at all. Think about the context as well as the problem itself. For more on context, see Chapter 10.

Groups and problems

The solution to a problem or the ways to address a new opportunity can also be shaped by who the issue is given to at the outset. A book-keeper or prison warder will probably arrive at a different solution from a poet or an artist. Different mindsets may view the issues in quite different ways. Generally speaking, diversity of opinion from within groups, when well managed, pays dividends. A wide range of views will ultimately produce more interesting solutions and opportunities. By inviting authoritative outsiders to give their view on a problem you can reduce the risk of developing the arrogance of 'NIH' (not invented here – where people resist new ideas). As ever, there is a balance to be struck. Too much diversity and expertise gets diluted out. Too much expertise and we end up with hybrid stupidity and NIH rules. (Hybrid stupidity is a term I picked up as a genetics student. The term refers to animals that have been bred for something highly specific. Quite often the pure form will exhibit serious shortcomings in other areas. Our observation was that variety, as opposed to purity, conferred the greatest biological advantage in the long term.)

In summary

Problems exist in a context, usually with some other baggage attached. Outcomes will also be determined partly by the mindset and ability of the person(s) who work on them. The quality of decisions when giving thought to a problem will depend on whether the problem is clear cut or slippery.

The sort of problems people in positions of authority most commonly encounter have a political aspect. Resolving this sort of problem requires the intellectual agility to balance the needs of different parties. In addition, when faced with slippery situations, the nature of the decision or solution will only remain valid for a limited period of time because the problem itself is often subject to substantial change. Getting various different opinions can help with the resolution of slippery problems.

Thinking about the nature of a problem *before* you attempt to work on it can save time and effort.

The glory of error: What if I make a mistake?

Error has a major impact on thinking, behaviour, expectations and performance. So we need to consider error. At all of my workshops I ask if that paragon of virtue who never makes mistakes is present among us.

If you are not making mistakes you are probably not doing very much.

Of course we will all make mistakes. This is very normal. So why do we make such a fuss about errors and mistakes? By definition, the higher in management we go the bigger our mistakes should be. Of course we should avoid foolish behaviour and we should not put fools in charge of complicated decisions, but once we have recruited great people to work for us, why do we expect their every decision and action to be error free?

One of the biggest binds I have seen managers get themselves into is for some strange reason to assume they are not allowed to make any mistakes. Perhaps they believe there is an unwritten rule that people who work for them expect no less. Once a belief about perfect performance takes hold, the concept becomes infectious. Managers and staff are then able to impose the same illogical idea of perfect performance, free of error, on others.

Great people make mistakes too!

Why do we persistently behave as if mistakes are a bad thing? The answer probably has something to do with assumptions about power, shame, guilt, failure and perhaps social fit within a group. We should remember that great people make great big mistakes too.

Young managers look up to those in positions of power. As a young manager, I personally 'expected' that any manager above me must, by virtue of their position, be better than me. I learned later how wrong this assumption was. If I expected my boss to be error free, it left me no room for error whatsoever. Later, as a general manager, I realized some of my young ambitious managers had the very same unreasonable error-free expectation of me!

Having worked hard to earn power, perhaps the fear of losing authority or the confidence of others by being shown to be in error makes us cover up. This prevents us from sharing useful knowledge about errors. We all like to know about the success pathways on life, but it is just as important to know where the swamps are too!

What if we changed 'the rules' about how we think and talk about error? We could then openly declare, '*Great*, we made a mistake. Now we know more!' If we made a virtue out of mistakes, then we could safely acknowledge we were creating knowledge of what to avoid. Further we could declare openly we were also discovering opportunities to learn. Our mistakes would also be a form of acknowledgement that we were taking enough decisions!

This suggestion may sound like 'pie in the sky' – or nonsense – but it does make sense. All that is required to make this work is a recognizable management context for safely displaying error.

Often we fail to reverse the prevailing (bad) logic that mistakes are personal and must be hidden because this is the way we all do things today. There is an unwritten rule that tacitly suggests, 'If I step out of line I will be exposed and become vulnerable', or in some countries 'shamed'. If we want to improve the general quality of thinking and behaviour, this belief will need to change in individuals and groups. If you employ great people and they give the job their best and fullest attention, then any error must be considered in a positive light.

Shame and guilt have no place in routine management. These terms should be reserved for explicitly evil acts and not for the everyday mistakes to which we are all prone.

The old rule sets about error are at work with groups of people in factories and offices just as they are within families. Because social values such as these exist tacitly, they are rarely exposed for examination or debate, despite the huge impact they have on the way we think and on our performance. We may also be unreasonably afraid of the consequences of challenging the old order. We should reconsider the way we think about error, mistakes and failure and change our perceptions for the better.

Failure is OK, failure is good

Dr William E. Coyne Sr, Research and Development Vice-President at 3M, says, 'We acknowledge that failure is part of life ... and we expect failure on a grand scale. For every 1000 raw ideas, only 100 are written up as formal proposals. Only a fraction of those become new product ventures. And more than half our new product ventures fail.'[1]

> **Knowledge should include error as a normal part of the learning process**

In another excellent example of changing attitudes about error, a former client published an internal website of major top-level management blunders in a 'graveyard' for all staff to see. Not only that, they classified types of mistakes into groups which they called the seven 'sins' so that other managers could learn from their collective history. Knowledge should include error as a normal part of the learning process. It should not be hidden, for the simple reason that in the absence of the knowledge we will repeat the error.

Tip Get the directors to get used to displaying their past errors, first to each other, then to a wider audience. Then get them to talk openly about their biggest learning events. Create your own stories about the journeys out of failure to success – and transmit them!

Another anecdote I really like is that of a young, hard-working executive who really took a dive on a computer contract. Let me express this another way – he really screwed up. Because of an error of judgement he lost his firm many millions of dollars. As soon as the error became apparent, he decided he would resign rather than wait to be fired. So the next Monday morning he presented his letter to the head of the business who said, 'Why would we want to let you go? We've just spent millions on your education!'

Some companies recognize that a simple reversal of outdated 'shame' beliefs associated with error can have a massive impact. A leading UK food group, for example, accepts a high failure rate as a normal part of the research process. They openly acknowledge a failure rate of 70 per cent in the development process of several thousand new products per year. Their message is that in order to innovate successfully, they must make lots and lots of errors, and have many low-cost failures, to get enough successes in the 30 per cent range.

Tip The grapevine is 1000 times more effective than the house magazine. If you want to send a clear message signalling tolerance of error, promote someone young with great potential but who recently failed. (Then coach, mentor and protect them.)

Risk and error: Two philosophies

There are two quite different approaches to action. 'Ready, Fire, Aim!' characterizes one while 'Simple masterful action preceded by deep quiet reflection' characterizes the other. The first might be described as extrovert and the latter as introvert.

The *general* orientation among groups with the former approach is to act first, think later. The second is a quite different, pensive, reflective approach. Within this alternative belief system, people think deeply and then, at the right moment, act with precision and apparently without fault. Perhaps there is an evolutionary reason for these two quite different particular patterns.

In some countries, society believes that the individual is important while in others the emphasis is on the needs of the community over the needs of the individual.

In societies where individualism is the prevailing force, people cannot rely on the larger population to protect them as individuals. Therefore under these conditions, when at risk, the probability for survival will be better if the individual moves early, quickly and with self-interest in mind, in anticipation of perceived risk. Such societies expect people to take care of themselves and the laws of the land may be biased towards the rights of the individual. Popular stories reflect the importance of individuals.

If the culture strongly promotes collective behaviour, risk to the individual is reduced. Society might in return expect the individual to protect the society first. Under these conditions, the laws will protect society from the individual. The collective can take time to study, learn and move with more confidence. A collective may be slow to respond but, when it does act, it will do so with a greater sense of certainty and confidence.

A collective may be slow to respond but, when it does act, it will do so with a greater sense of certainty and confidence

Individualism may be favoured in hostile, fast-changing environments and collectivism in relatively stable environments. The latter needs time to create consensus and will be less efficient in rapidly changing markets. The only way collective systems will catch up with the individualistic societies in fast-moving environments is to find a way of adopting very fast consensus mechanisms or to develop a fundamentally new collective frame of reference.

Given the fundamental differences in the two major operating paradigms, it appears unlikely that a wholesale movement of one philosophy to the other could ever happen. If this is so, misunderstanding and conflict between the two are predictable. Let's now consider the impact on thinking of the two philosophies, which may create two quite different attitudes to decision making and error.

Individualism: Extrovert culture

Extroverts act early, trip up, recover quickly, learn and move on.

The overall group orientation is essentially outward facing and fast acting. Time spent initially in thinking, exploring and studying detail or on reflection is relatively low. The core belief is about exceptional 'individuals' working in teams. This is carried to its extreme with the idea of huge organizations being led by one exceptional CEO.

This bias for early action in the extrovert culture model matches the predominantly focused thinking or convergent model outlined in Chapter 2. When we use mostly convergent or focused thinking there tends to be little if no reflection initially. Only after problems persist or as new problems emerge is further thought applied.

Extrovert problem solving

Let's imagine a group of managers from an extrovert culture who are considering how much stock to hold for multiple lines of food or fashion products in a fast-moving market. Estimates vary considerably as to how often managers' decisions are correct. Just for the purpose of the current exercise, let's assume they have a 33 per cent success rate (the specific figure used is irrelevant to the exercise as it is the general pattern that we will be focusing upon). The decision making of our retail managers thus leads to approximately one-third of the stock being in excess, one-third below ideal levels and another third on target. Now let's plot their decision path on to a chart.

An extrovert model of progress

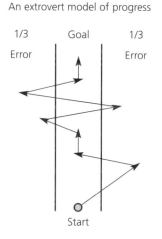

This gives us a model that throws up some interesting positions that we can now make explicit. For instance, let's consider an experienced middle manager in an extrovert culture who is aware that brand new, original decisions are, two times out of three, more likely to be wrong than right. What behaviour might he or she adopt?

There are only three choices of interpretation and behaviour:

- Firmly resist any change because we know from the evidence that new decisions do not work nearly 70 per cent of the time! Produce the evidence and precedents to justify heavy resistance to change.

- Comply with change requests and get ready to blame someone else.

- Acknowledge that errors will happen and learn as we progress.

Mistakes can be thought of as useful lessons or interesting opportunities

One contributory reason why some decisions actually work is that each time we fail, we learn where not to look or act next time. The more we make mistakes as we continue to push at solving a problem, the more likely we will hit on something useful. In other words, decision making is iterative, meaning we learn as we practise. Mistakes can be thought of as useful lessons or interesting opportunities. The more decisions we take, the higher the chance of learning. With each step we increase the chance of getting it right in the end. So if managers from extrovert cultures are to learn how to think smarter, disclosure of error, learning and moving on are essential.

But how do people in extrovert organizations *actually* behave when they make a mistake? Actually, it is not unusual for them to hide an error, work late and then declare triumphantly how they single-handedly fixed a problem over the weekend. What heroes! When a person actively hides a problem from wider attention, huge amounts of energy will be dissipated in trying to solve the problem alone without the resources available in a wider group. Imagine the enormous waste of time and effort involved when this narrow, selfish approach to problem solving is practised across a large organization. Think how much faster an organization could work if error was considered OK and not career threatening.

Some problems don't get fixed, of course, and cover-ups lead to even bigger problems later. Occasionally this leads to severe difficulties.

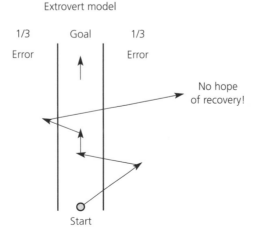

Extrovert model

If a manager isn't making many mistakes, he or she probably isn't making enough decisions

An extreme case involving hundreds of millions of dollars' worth of foreign currency losses sank one of Britain's oldest banks because one individual allegedly hid errors in the hope that he could make good his losses.

What is worth thinking about is: why do people in the extrovert model cover up and hide their mistakes and errors? What is their motivation behind error avoidance and cover-up? If most managers have a similar error rate, one might reasonably assume that management mistakes must be commonplace enough for the subject to be safely acknowledged. Put another way, if a manager isn't making many mistakes, he or she probably isn't making enough decisions – so why don't we talk about errors, mistakes and failure more often?

> **Tip** When you have a reasonable quota of your own success stories to act as a counter-balance, sharing your bigger errors with colleagues is likely to be warmly accepted, especially if well presented. This sort of behaviour increases learning and, if well managed, can increase a sense of trust. If you are a leader it can also promote a shift in the culture away from blame.

Powerful humility

When you think it through, the logic in support of the desire for error-free decision making in extrovert environments sounds reasonable when actually it is not. Error-free decision making is an impossible position to sustain, especially with the increasing complexity of issues. So how might we adopt a different approach to dealing with the way we think about errors and mistakes? One of the greatest assets a manager in authority can possess is humility. Humility is a huge asset that has impact beyond the immediately obvious. To be able to admit your own mistakes and laugh at them is to show your humanity. Well-placed expressions of humility also make you appear more approachable and more forgiving. Humility can make you stronger inside too, because you have the confidence to forgive yourself.

Of course there is a balance to be struck between looking human and overplaying the asset and looking foolish! The point is, it is not wise or healthy to be *always* in control, and always correct. There is a balance here too.

Tip Learn to laugh when you make a mistake: it improves both your sense of well-being and your learning. Be prepared to share the laughter with others occasionally: it provides relief from tension and permission to change.

Tip Put error on your management agenda as a positive learning opportunity. Try to make error exposure fun so that any negative tension can be dissipated in a positive way. The goal is to promote earlier, full disclosure.

Tip Be clear about what level of error constitutes the forgivable and the unforgivable.

Within extrovert communities, as individuals we want to excel in our organization. We want people to appreciate us for the good things we do, so perhaps we might choose to hide our less than successful work, hoping we can surf the promotion system, remaining ahead of our own errors. This personal strategy clearly benefits the individual but not the organization. Learning is reduced and errors may remain hidden too long. A whole range of people may see error disclosure as a sign of weakness or perhaps a way of losing promotion prospects. In order to correct this a major change in culture has to be developed.

Tip Review the way you empower or disempower people. Is there a gap between what you want and what you actually get? Do you personally make it safe for your people to talk about error? Consider the way the most common conversations are played out. Perhaps you could try a process of role reversal – add some humour as a safety net and see what responses surface.

This model of decision making might be described as naive, since there is a degree of trust, confidence and faith that 'the answer is out there', but for the same reasons an extrovert culture is essentially optimistic.

Assuming that there is only one current philosophy in operation could be fatal in business

The extrovert culture is one that many of us will immediately recognize. However, as we have already said, it is not the only one, and it would be dangerous to assume that it was. Assuming that there is only one current philosophy in operation and that we are all thinking in the same way could be fatal in business, in war or in the increasing number of cross-cultural relationships within the global business community.

Collectivism: Introvert culture

Introvert cultures value quite different things from extrovert cultures.

An alternative view of reality

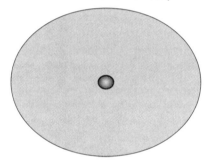

The way of thinking in this introvert culture model begins with the idea that strength and reliance come from within 'one'. The approach is holistic, the thinking is Zen-like. Everything outside the self must be assumed to be hostile and dangerous especially if unknown or not yet mastered. The starting point may appear to be essentially pessimistic, but it leads on to the suggestion that true security can only be gained by knowing oneself deeply and by surrounding oneself with stable, long-term, loyal relationships that are firmly bound together by responsibility or other bonds. Ultimately only strong groups survive. Groups are more important than the individual. Once one is a member of such a group, behaviour is highly inclusive. Sharing is expected and consensus is the norm. As a consequence 'variances', problems and opportunity can be discussed within the group.

In the illustration above, the starting point – an individual, a small group or an issue – is represented by a small dot in the centre of the larger circle of a problem or market. *In this model a person perceives that completion or the correct answer lies at the edge of the circle.* Individuals must be discreet along the journey. They must hide their weakness *and* their power, move only when they are certain of mastery. Not trusting outsiders is regarded as the most reasonable starting point. The collective face you show the outside world should not give away anything you do not wish to share.

An alternative view of security

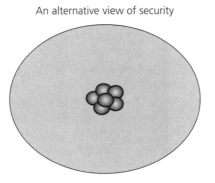

In the absence of knowledge of how to reach the edge in this model, one seeks to surround oneself with long-lasting relationships and to steadily but discreetly acquire the missing knowledge. In knowledge and loyal relationships lies strength. Resolution of the issue will be achieved when the edge of the circle is reached, in a few masterstrokes.

An alternative view of strength

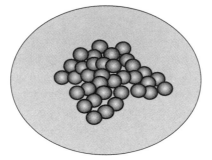

When the gap between you (collectively) and the edge is quickly bridgeable, one decisive leap is made. Thus, when viewed by an extrovert organization from outside the circle, nothing tangible seems to be happening within this type of company until suddenly, with apparently remarkable speed, efficiency and accuracy, the introvert organization homes in on its goal.

An alternative view of
how to progress

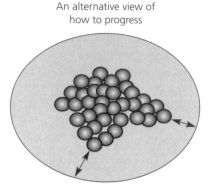

It is interesting to try to view each perception through the other's eyes, using the insights from the two models above. Extrovert culture managers working with those from an introvert culture wonder why their counterparts appear so quiet, relatively inactive and almost insular. By contrast, the reaction of introvert culture managers might be one of alarm to see their extrovert culture counterparts blundering from one mistake to another without thinking or preparation!

The introvert model has its benefits and its drawbacks. The consensus management system, where everyone has to be seen to agree, enables consistent high quality to be delivered within predictable environments. Commitment to acquiring and openly sharing information internally should enable such companies to reduce inefficiencies at a relatively higher rate than their counterparts; the individualistic employees of extrovert cultures might not be as willing to share errors, difficulties or incremental improvements.

On the other hand, the introvert culture approach can be very slow and tends not to be too dynamic when faced with quickly changing environments. Also the forces at work here reward cohesion of the whole community *above* individuality. Reversing a decision could become a nightmare, especially when multiple consensus groups have approved and contributed to the accuracy and correctness of the first decision. Another drawback of this approach, its attitude to dissenting views, is well illustrated in the Japanese saying, 'If a nail stands up, strike it down!' A personal survival strategy in this environment, therefore, is not to say anything so one cannot be seen to be incorrect and thus ridiculed or shamed. This makes it highly unlikely that purely original thought will originate from such confines.

'Don't argue with the teacher' is another free-thought block in some communities. If teachers and elders are to be greatly respected, this might be considered as great news when obedience and compliance are wanted.

In times of war or in factories that demand repetitive compliance, obedience and cohesion are valuable assets. This sort of strict structure makes for high efficiency in situations where the information is mostly known but needs refining. However, such behaviours and beliefs, where the old order cannot be challenged, do nothing to aid developing truly original thinking, new ideas or knowledge.

The earth would forever have remained flat if we all adhered to the beliefs of all those who came before us

The earth would forever have remained flat if we all adhered to the beliefs of all those who came before us.

At heart I'm still a biologist. I strongly believe that nature loves diversity and dislikes narrow, pure, relatively simplistic systems, so I would expect exceptions and contradictions to exist within my two simple introvert and extrovert models for error. These models are far from pure but nevertheless are useful generalizations.

As a reader, you might perhaps associate introvert cultures with organizations in the Far East. This would be wrong. From personal experience I have seen this sort of pattern with a large German company, and associates who work in different parts of Asia describe patterns more akin to those seen in the USA and Britain. If you are interested in cultural differences, see the substantial body of work by Fons Trompenaars and Charles Hampden-Turner.

Hybrids

As I mentioned above, nature loves diversity. A curious mix of the introvert and extrovert models of approach to error exists in Danish philosophy, which demands that an individual look within themselves for answers and not rely on others and gives explicit acknowledgement to ten rules written in the 1900s by author Aksel Sandemose in his book *En flygtning krysser sitt spor*, that is, 'A Refugee Crosses His Own Shadow'. The book is set in an imaginary Danish small town called Jante. The story line is about the ugly aspects of Scandinavian small-town mentality, and the term 'Janteloven', meaning 'the Jante Laws', has come to refer to the unspoken rules of some communities in Denmark.

Most Danes are aware of these Jante Laws. They are not enforced in any explicit, formal way but knowledge of them helps Danes understand how their communities actually work. The rules are as follows and, as you will see, they are far from soft (I am indebted to two friends in Denmark for their translation):

1 You shall not presume that you are anyone.

2 You shall not presume that you are as good as us.

3 You shall not venture to think that you are any wiser than we are.

4 You shall never indulge in the conceit of imagining that you are better than us.

5 You shall not presume that you are more knowledgeable than we are.

6 You shall not venture to think that you are more than we are.

7 You shall not presume that you are going to amount to anything.

8 You are not entitled to laugh at us.

9 Never imagine that anyone cares about you.

10 Do not suppose that you can teach us anything.

The intellectual energy released by the clash between open and extrovert Viking thinking and the harsh Jante Laws may perhaps account for the disproportionately high level of innovation, design excellence and creative activity from a nation of only five million people.

Denmark has many contradictions. The most curious is perhaps the biggest, namely the contrast between the self-reliance demanded by the Jante Laws and the high levels of taxation (circa 65 per cent) coupled with a very socialist, caring state provision for ill health and unemployment. Perhaps we should look at Denmark as a Zen state with a safety net! People earn a lot of money there and hand most of it back to the state. Elegantly thrifty, aesthetically aware and extremely productive, Danes continue to produce a disproportionately high number of good ideas. It seems contradiction well handled works.

Value systems

Can a prevailing culture in society affect the way we think and work? I would propose that it can. But philosophy that merely allows academics to tie each other up in grammatical knots serves no useful purpose. If we are to develop useful ideas about how we can live better lives, the concepts must ultimately be pragmatic, easy to understand and accessible to a large number of people. As with 'thinking', we rarely examine the philosophies or value systems that we adopt or inherit. Perhaps we would rather not even begin to think about such subjects and let someone else tell us their answer. If that approach is not a moral risk, I don't know what is! If we are going to live and work by a set of rules or beliefs, we should actively think through why we should or should not accept them.

Perhaps in this millennium, as life becomes increasingly complicated, where our value systems are challenged or seen wanting, some people will pay more attention to the simple, basic elements of life in an effort to retrieve quality based upon simplicity. How you think is a start.

Tip If you had to write down your own rules for life what would they be? Write them down and refine them over time. Where or what are your signposts and stop signs? Personal values are deeply held and if you go against them the quality of your thinking will waiver. If you want to conquer yourself, understanding these rules will be an important aid to clarifying your thought about your life's mission. Have you thought about what your life mission is? Is it worthy? Energy and vigour, or the lack of them, are sometimes a consequence of the extent to which you are aligned with your own good values and personal mission.

Error, curiosity and serendipity

From the outside the prevailing paradigm in Japan appears to be efficient at exploiting the realms of the known and persistently refining it to ever higher standards. Where their belief system seems to be much less efficient is in dealing with the unknown. The major advances in leading-edge sciences such as biotechnology, pharmaceuticals, microelectronics and software have mostly evolved in countries such as Britain, the USA and more recently Germany. One reason for this is perhaps the relatively chaotic approach adopted for problem solving in these last-named countries, together with a healthy disrespect by rebel individuals for rules or historical precedent. Such chaos and disrespect lend themselves nicely to serendipity. Serendipity is 'a happy accident'. Serendipity happens when things are loose, not when they are tightly controlled.

> **Serendipity happens when things are loose, not when they are tightly controlled**

... we do believe in discipline ... but at the same time 3M management encourages a healthy disrespect for 3M management. This is not the sort of thing we publicise in our annual report, but the

> stories we tell ... with relish ... are frequently about 3Mers who
> have circumvented their superiors and succeeded.
>
> DR W.E. COYNE, 3M[2]

Curious minds, as opposed to disciplined minds, consider odd findings and apparent errors to be a major source repository for 'future interesting stuff'. This way of thinking enables serendipity to occur.

Sometimes curiosity turns into an obsessive belief, if not a passion, and years later a revolutionary product or process emerges. For example, there are two recent particular products that do not fit the usual R&D pattern of applied meticulous science. Both are classics.

The first is the clockwork radio, a British invention. This is a lovely example of an abstract invention.

The other is Viagra™, a new drug for sexual dysfunction in older men and women. This is an example of serendipity or, as some would say, an 'accidental' discovery. Viagra™ was discovered in Britain for an American company. Sales ran to millions of dollars per day only a few months after its launch and Viagra™ is set to become a blockbuster billion-dollar money maker, but – and here's the serendipity – it was originally developed as a heart drug, at which clinical trials showed it was a failure! Viagra™'s success as a sexual aid was not designed or deduced; it was pure serendipity, pure chance. The product should have been consigned to the failure file, but an individual employee chose to investigate closely with individual trial subjects as to why they were so slow to return trial samples after the original heart trial was stopped. Curiosity and serendipity combined and produced an outstanding commercial success for the company.

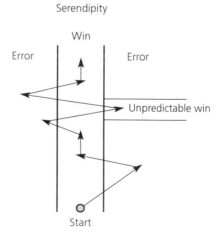

Serendipity

Unpredictable wins, gains based on happy accidents, can be immensely valuable. The last century had very many of them, starting with penicillin, which can trace its origins to a simple mistake.

If the Viagra™ team of pharmaceutical scientists had relied solely on pure logic, they could easily have decided, 'This potential heart drug has failed along with many in our programme. Consign it to the fail file; put it in the bin.' In the relentless quest to find the next blockbuster product, a billion-dollar money spinner would have been unwittingly consigned to the trash can. So what makes the difference that allows someone to 'see' the upside possibilities in an unexpected result when someone else would not have given these massive opportunities a second thought?

> **Penicillin can trace its origins to a simple mistake**

In order for serendipity or abstract approaches to work, people who can think with open, curious minds are essential. They are the ones who can see or sense the positive potential of an error.

To be able to exploit serendipity, the way we think about error has to move from one of negative concern to one of positive excitement and

Fostering the right stuff

Some people tend not to be good at sharing their problems and will tend to stew in them internally rather than share them openly with others. This behaviour is going to have to change if society is to remain healthy and wealthy. Internalizing or stewing in a problem, without sharing it, promotes a pattern of non-disclosure of errors and problems. Life both at work and at home is getting too fast and too complicated for this to remain acceptable. Also, the impact of undisclosed errors or problems is growing faster than an individual's ability to cope. Men in particular, since they have a tendency to this sort of behaviour, are going to have to find new ways of resolving complexities.

Some old management ideas on leadership are going to have to change too. For example, encouraging decision making in junior managers by saying, 'Don't bring me problems, bring solutions' may actually foster the wrong behaviour of hiding problems. We might actually believe that what we have said will give people an empowered position, but what might be heard is, 'You're on your own, kid!' Clearly we are going to have to review what we say and do to motivate people to perform well in a complex future, especially in situations where we need to fail sometimes in order to know what to avoid later.

curiosity about what else this could lead to. Being ready for serendipity in the way we think is one dimension of an orientation towards being innovative.

What we should say when presented with odd information is, 'Great, a new opportunity!' What gets in the way of celebrating happy accidents, useful errors and serendipity is the way we are encouraged to think and sometimes base motivations such as fear, a need for power, ego mainte-nance or self-protection.

> Error is not error; it is simply more information.
> 'Error' is an attitude.

In summary

So error is not all bad. In fact, used properly, error can be really good. Someone's error is simply another guidepost and as such is potentially interesting to other people. Error is not wasted effort. Error is knowledge, just as correct information is. Knowing where the territory is swampy is just as important as knowing the correct road. Error is an opportunity. Error is to be flagged and celebrated, on balance, alongside success. Working through our errors often prepares us for something bigger and better later on in life, as long as we are ready to learn to improve and to adapt the way we think and behave.

So the attitude to how information fits or does not fit into a pattern in our individual and our collective consciousness is very important. Having the right collective mindset, particularly with regard to error, determines whether a breakthrough, a quantum-leap discovery, is possible or not with individual or team effort.

In management we frequently have to take decisions quickly or with incomplete information. Often there is a strong element of ambiguity in our decision making. Dealing effectively with ambiguity is one of those qualities that rarely appear on the job appraisal form, yet it is a very nec-essary thinking skill. The next chapter looks at ambiguity and what sort of thinking tools, concepts or images we might employ to help us when deal-ing with ambiguous information.

Notes

[1, 2] Source: *The UK Innovation Lecture, 5/3/96: Building a Tradition of Innovation*, DTI Booklet URN 96/619.

Ambiguity: Living in a foggy landscape

8

Our ability to cope with ambiguity and its effect on thinking

Modern life, generally speaking, is far from simple. We now live in an age where we are more likely to receive too much information than too little. In addition, the level of complexity and speed of change are increasing all the time. Anyone or any process that remains relatively slow risks being pushed down the economic food chain. Even when we try to simplify matters, something unexpected often arrives to confound us! Perhaps we are not supposed to 'arrive'. While we paddle or sail through our complex lives, we will frequently need to deal with a variety of conflicting ideas or issues, often at the same time. Dealing with complex issues requires intellectual agility and flexibility as well as a faculty for using partial or contradictory information. In evolutionary terms, we will have to learn how to flex our minds, in order to survive the relentless demands placed upon all of us to change and then change again. In short, an ability to deal with ambiguity is increasingly needed by people from all levels of an organization and particularly by senior managers.

Perhaps society's resistance to teaching intellectual flexibility thus far may be a concern that such 'loose thinking' will lead to some sort of Bohemian impoverishment or immorality. That may well have been a relevant argument in the past, but the scope for the employment of creative, flexible minds in industries of the future is set to rise dramatically as complexity increases.

The nature of world trade is shifting rapidly too. The information and high-technology age is giving birth to new, creative, knowledge-intensive industries and revitalizing old ones. For example, the film production industry is set to rise dramatically in England as Hollywood loosens its grip on servicing a global market. What was once a dead-in-the-water British industry is beginning to make a comeback. On the other hand, however, as English becomes the language of world media, science and business, we may increasingly find that one of the world's largest communities of computer programmers lives not in Silicon Valley but in India. In addition, education and entertainment are making more use of creative media, in many languages. So, avoiding ambiguity, contradiction and complexity will be increasingly difficult for those who choose to live within wealthy societies. The rules are both global and local at the same time.

Thus, given the changing nature of global information flows and the fast-moving dynamic needs of employers, teaching people *how* to think and how to deal with ambiguity may turn out to be more relevant than pounding ordered information into the heads of our students. Otherwise they will be ill prepared not only for the content but even for the nature of what constitutes work in the future.

The most basic step in dealing with ambiguity is to be able to suspend judgement and to allow the existence of separate concepts and ideas. In the course of this chapter I will discuss four image tools I use to help people with this, namely:

- Yin–Yang
- elastic tension
- 'splits graphs'
- 'bubble thinking'.

All are image based, for good reason. By keeping images in mind when thinking about concepts, we can enrich our thoughts and bed down ideas much faster than with words alone.

Yin and Yang

Yin–Yang
In the Yin–Yang model two equal and opposing major forces are constantly at work. They are intimately connected and inseparable. In Chapter 6 Yin–Yang was employed to describe different problem types.

We also saw that the image is 'alive' and can rotate. The idea that the whole rotates also keeps in mind our need to constantly review decisions and our reference points to see if they remain relevant. Neither of the two major forces can be cancelled out. Also the essential character of each force contains an element of the other. This image is useful when dealing with ambiguity because it suggests that incomplete, optimal positions are the most likely outcome in ambiguous situations.

An example of thinking that fits a Yin–Yang model would be the idea 'In times of peace prepare for war and in times of war prepare for peace'.

Another good ambiguity I use in my thinking skills workshops is:

Your greatest strength is also your greatest weakness.

Ambiguity and elasticity

Imagine someone is required to run between two fixed points. Around the runner's waist are tied two elastic cords, each of which is also anchored at one of the two fixed points, say 100 metres apart. As our runner runs towards one fixed point, or anywhere else for that matter, there will be a force pulling backwards. There may well be a point at which tension is lowest for our runner. If the point of lowest tension happens to be undesirable then the only way to get to a desired place, given the constraints, is to put in the effort and live with the tension. Managing ambiguity can be viewed as a battle to balance opposing forces. One can either suffer the tension that ambiguity creates or learn to enjoy it. Some people I know seek out ambiguity as a rich source of amusement while others avoid it.

> **Managing ambiguity can be viewed as a battle to balance opposing forces**

Ambiguity and leverage points

When faced with a mess of complex issues, one approach is to try to find the origin, the nexus or the focal points within the complexity. Sometimes there may be a small number of pivotal issues that exert disproportionate influence. Rather than deal with all the dimensions, look for leverage points. If the whole issue can be rendered simple, it can often be easier to deal with. Complexity may sometimes be a case of an error of perception. There are occasions when a simple solution is exactly what is needed. Being 'bull headed' sometimes pays off.

> **Tip** *The Gordian Knot.* This was a huge rope knot that was presented as a challenge to Alexander the Great. The oracles of the time said, 'He who unties the knot will conquer Asia.' The knot was so complex that it would have been extremely difficult to untie. Rather than struggle, Alexander simply chose to use a mighty swing of the sword to cleave the knot apart. Sometimes this may be the best approach to complexity – if you don't value the rope.

Remember, though, that in dealing with complexity, absolute influence and pure outcomes will be rare. Once you accept that the outcomes may be partial, a resolution may be easier to find.

The splits

Have you ever tried to do what gymnasts call the splits? It is painful but possible. Doing the splits easily is really only possible after a lot of training and exercises aimed at stretching normally taut sinews to go that bit further. A few people can do it, but the rest of us can go only some way before a pain barrier stops us hurting ourselves.

People and organizations are much the same when it comes to dealing with ambiguity. Most managers are familiar with the need to balance conflicting priorities with multiple demands upon limited resources. In any organization there will be more good ideas than resources to deliver them, more problems than available people to solve them, and never enough time. Often these forces will be in contradiction with one another, creating a tension.

These tensions are very real. Often you can actually sense them. People holding powerful positions of authority in organizations can get quite passionate about their beliefs about what is correct and will frequently engage in conflict with equally passionate people who hold the opposite view. Both views will have validity and create tension. In physical terms, tension is a consequence of forces acting in different directions upon something else. We can sketch a simple map of such forces at work, making it easy to predict a variety of outcomes. The following series of shapes are just such maps. They can be just as easily reinterpreted for personal relationships.

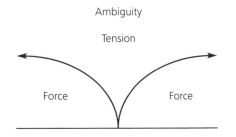

There is a whole range of contradictory forces at work within a business and institutions. It is entirely possible to be successful with different levels of emphasis on differing priorities. In other words, there is no such thing as a formula for success. The organizations that are more likely to be successful longer will be those that manage more contradictions. Where conversations are equally entertained from lists A *and* B below there will be more scope for variety and for evolution to occur. Life is neither pure nor absolute. Nor is life within an organization.

Conversations A	Conversations B
Control	Experiment
Cut costs	Gain bigger budgets
Just in time	New product development
Business process re-engineering	New business development
Total quality management	Research and development
Risk avoidance	Let's try something new
Financial engineering	Building a business
Budgets	Dreams

A simple example of tension in many companies is the drive to improve profitability by cutting costs versus the drive to stay in front of the competition by bringing out new products and services or by doing something innovative, i.e. spending more money.

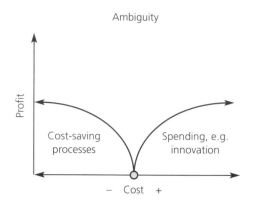

As with humans attempting to do the splits, organizations have tolerance levels too. If there is too much tension, damage occurs. Organizations therefore adopt self-defence mechanisms. Some defence mechanisms will be clear and explicit while others may be hidden, subtle or tacit.

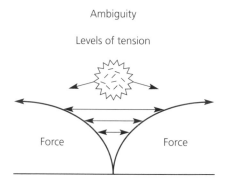

Too much tension can be bad for an organization. However, if there is too little tension, things go flaccid!

The key to dealing effectively with ambiguity is not to attempt to drive it out of the system but to accept that there will always be tension at work and that this can be harnessed. The trick is to place and maintain effective limits to keep tension high enough but not so high that damage occurs. As a consequence people need conflict skills. Sometimes the balance can slip, as the next chart suggests.

In this case, tension forces may well have been identified and limits put in place, but one side has pulled too far and dominated the other; they have won, but the organization may have lost. The match is not an equal one. In

Ambiguity &
desirable tension
(i) No tension, dominance

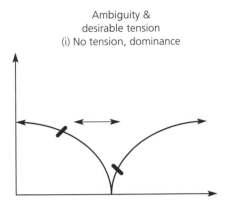

effect there is no real tension since one force is totally dominated by the other. The power of ambiguity has been lost. Life is simpler but less rich. There will be a myopic sense of clarity but little vision and poor motivation.

The chart below is an illustration where the two opposing forces are either too constrained or perhaps too polite to develop real tension. Again life is relatively simple and unchallenged here. There may be a sense of frustration or of resignation, or even odd game playing to avoid tension.

Ambiguity &
desirable tension
(ii) Stalemate

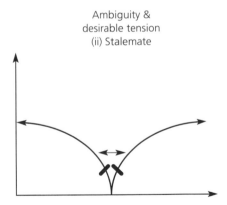

Essentially this is a flaccid situation. There is no power, no sense of tension. The edicts and words are there, but the power to move has been muted. Inspiration happens only outside of the organization.

In doing the splits, a little pain is necessary in order to know where the current limits are. Stretch is required to get up to and beyond those limits if we wish to grow. When we get lazy or when we fail to

In doing the splits, a little pain is necessary

grow we can end up feeling lifeless and without the vitality of our youth. This can happen when we are faced with increasingly familiar difficulties that become easier to deal with. This applies just as much in our personal lives as it does at work. Sometimes we need to change something dramatically or challenge ourselves in a vivid way in order to remind us we are alive. One manager I met years ago proposed that, in order to invigorate your life, you should do something that puts you in close touch with raw nature. As I write this book I have just witnessed on TV a woman over the age of 70 landing in harness after a tandem parachute jump! I would say the tension was back in her life! Wow! As far as I can see, she will have pushed the limits on her assumptions about what is and is not possible. The point I am making is that sometimes the lack of tension is due to the assumptions we carry within ourselves or an inability to manage conflict.

A desirable situation is to be in a position of matched contradictions where the outer and the inner limits are known and maintained. If these contradictory forces are ever relaxed or increased then this must be a conscious considered action.

Ambiguity &
desirable tension
(iii) Balanced contradiction

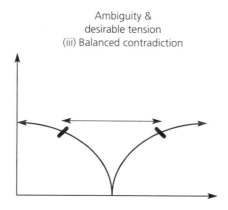

3M

A good example of managed tensions exists within a global diversified company called 3M, which innovates relentlessly. This American company is well known for the way it manages to drive a wide range of innovations out of its core technologies. The progress of 3M is all the more remarkable when one considers its relatively simple origins in industrial adhesive tapes and abrasive papers. Boring products, you might well say. Well, 3M is anything but dull because it has a tightly managed yet intellectually rebellious culture. 3M staff manage contradictions such as this extremely well.

3M is synonymous with innovation. What is remarkable about this company is that it manages to extract novel applications from products with humble beginnings. For example, in considering abrasive papers used to flatten and smooth surfaces, 3M discovered that traditional sandpapers, when viewed under a microscope, had highly irregular sharp shapes that did the smoothing work. Their technologists thought it might be useful to produce highly regular, prism-shaped surfaces so that a more predictable smoothing job could be produced. Because the old papers were prone to clogging as a result of the irregular-shaped abrasive particles used to make the paper, the new approach would mean the new abrasive papers would last longer and wear down more evenly. This allowed 3M to sell a higher-priced, higher-margin product that worked out cheaper for the user than conventional abrasive papers. The company didn't stop there, though. Once it had mastered the ability to produce highly regular shapes and to lay these neatly on a surface, someone suggested this could improve airflow over the wings of aircraft. This in turn would reduce fuel consumption, so product development and sales began there. This application has been further adapted to include customized colourful designs. In addition someone else suggested that, if the regular prism shapes were transparent, light could travel through them over great distances. With this in mind, 3M set about producing flexible light tubes that could pipe light into a variety of indoor and roadside applications. This example shows how 3M thinks: from sandpaper to better abrasive papers, slipstream coatings on aircraft and light-tubes. And the development of the basic technology has not stopped there.

New products at 3M are researched within contradictions such as that of 'loose–tight' guidelines. 3M encourages a loose grip on R&D, allowing individual researchers to allocate 15 per cent of their time and budget at their own discretion. At the same time, 3M tightly manages its patents and expects its technologists to spend lots of time talking openly with customers about ideas and to spread their discoveries internally across a variety of other divisions. 3M manages the contradiction of open access and tight control. Influence at 3M is about how widely an idea is adopted and how much the system is 'bucked'. Tension is maintained between tight managerial control and intelligent rebellion.

Yet another contradiction is managed: old, familiar, reliable, profitable products have to be managed alongside new, unfamiliar, uncertain, unprofitable upstarts.

3M manages the contradiction of open access and tight control

Recognizing the nature of its markets' attrition rate, 3M sets as targets for their business managers to have 30 per cent of sales coming from recent innovations introduced within the last four years and 10 per cent within the last year.

Managing a variety of contradictions has helped build company and shareholder profitability in otherwise mundane markets and has sustained the pioneering character of the organization for over 90 years.

3M is not alone in considering the importance of applied contradiction.

Polarities

During the course of preparing material for this book I had a conversation with a Swedish international management development manager at one of Europe's leading pharmaceutical organizations. He agreed with my view that the ability to effectively manage ambiguity is beginning to be acknowledged as a valuable skill, but he preferred the term 'managing polarities'. Intrigued, I was led by further research to discover that the idea of Polarity Management™ was originated by an American author, Barry Johnson, who first published his concepts in 1992 and again in 1996.[1] Barry's concept of Polarity Management™ looks promising because his approach to dealing with quite complex problems has the clarity of common sense. Like a great many innovations, his ideas appear so obvious you are left wondering why you hadn't seen them for yourself long ago.

In his point of view there are basic problems which lend themselves to a definite solution and then, as the central thesis is Barry's work, there is a whole family of issues that do not lend themselves to 'either/or' decision making. These Barry calls 'Polarities', that is pairs of what might initially look like competing choices or diametrically opposed problems. A clear definite 100 per cent decision using binary either/or logic is *not* possible with a polarity. Polarities therefore need to be dynamically *managed* as opposed to decided upon because there can be no clear absolutre answer to or resolution of a polarity. Further more, with polarities, there is a dependency operating between two polar opposites. When a series of decisions is taken over time in an attempt to resolve a polarized pair, the consequences of past decision making will have the characteristics of an infinity loop moving between the extremes.

Each pole has clear advantages and disadvantages. If you find yourself in the negative aspects of one of the poles, for example, negative Alpha in the diagram below, then the positive aspects of the other option will present an attraction. Make the case for a transition to a far better place and then discover the disadvantages of Omega. Now the upsides of Alpha look like the right place to be after all! And so the cycle repeats the same figure-of-eight pattern, looping diagonally one way, then the other.

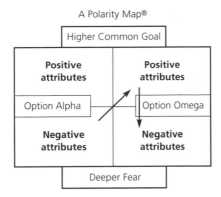

A Polarity Map®

Polarity Map™ reproduced with the permission of Barry Johnson

There are several layers of perception that stop us from resolving this repeating pattern. The first is that our minds often find it difficult to capture the whole picture. Secondly, we find it difficult or we do not know how to leave a decision 'open'; that is to say we like to close off an ambiguity in favour of a defined, clear, yes/no-type decision. A third barrier is that we fail to see that the two sides, because they are intimately connected, require simultaneous management. Deny one side of the equation and it hurts the other.

Situations which cannot be clearly resolved might include trying to decide whether to centralize or decentralize. Barry's methods suggest that we cannot resolve this sort of problem with a 'decision', simply because a polarity is never closed. We can, however,

> **Deny one side of the equation and it hurts the other**

manage them in a significantly better way than by attempting a closed decision. The solution lies in involving all the relevant parties, mapping the positives and negatives of each, openly acknowledging *all* of these and then, instead of making an either/or choice, attempting to do the best of both while at the same time working to minimize their worst effects. This requires clear models *and* the ability to deal effectively with ambiguity. For more on Barry's models and concepts, I suggest you refer to his book, *Polarity Management*™ (see recommended reading at the end of the book).

Perhaps by getting people to use the idea of working with 'polarities' rather than trying to choose between contradictions we can foster more of a win–win mindset and avoid the notion of losing when scarce resources are allocated.

Applied contradiction, agitation and tension

Some leaders believe that a state of perpetual tension is needed to heighten the energy level of a competitive organization. If this is true, then we might consider how this is achieved in a positive way. There is a risk in a competitive environment of creating winners and losers. Sometimes this is productive, at other times divisive. Perhaps in tussles for resources we should reward people who *fail* to win the argument but who successfully create and contribute to useful tension.

Every wave needs a rock to splash upon to prove itself a wave.

One manager I know made a career as a known agitator for the good of the organization. Eventually he became affectionately known as 'The Corporate Irritant'. Wise kings of old placed a high value on the wit and guile of a fool who would provoke good cause for thought. Several years ago, I met a senior manager from a top British-based global organization who had actually secured the official job title 'Corporate Jester'.

The practicalities of managing ambiguity

Often new ideas are postulated and quickly killed off for apparently good and valid reasons. However, to be effective in producing original ideas, one must resist such temptations and keep even faulty ideas alive long enough to bring life forth out of them. In other words, one must learn to entertain an ambiguous situation. One of the clients of my Innovation Forum maintains a place they call the 'greenhouse' specifically for this reason. In addition one must learn not only to suspend judgement but also to welcome the tension created by contradictions arising from the most ridiculous ideas. Often the more outrageous notions are the most productive source of later inspiration.

The biggest difficulties in delivering new ideas are not in development. Often that is the easy part. The most difficult aspects of any innovative venture are in dealing with a raft of contradictions, ambiguities and incomplete situations. New ideas are weak because they lack history, precedents; they are naked, and lack a frame of reference. For this reason, when they are placed in conflict with the old order, the outcome is very, very predictable. The old order will provide solid evidence and apparent clarity and certainty to challenge the unknown.

In situations where people are averse to risk, the old order invariably wins. To survive, the new must go somewhere else altogether or be isolated and totally protected from the old order.

It is very easy to kill off the new while it exists in an embryonic state

If we are ever to do anything original, the new situation must be allowed to begin in an environment without rules or established ways of doing things. This is research at its purest. The new will exist in a state of temporary ambiguity until the new rules become clear. It is very easy to kill off the new while it exists in an embryonic state.

Some people will kill off the new simply because it produces anxiety and uncertainty, while others will see it as a very real threat and will attack with vigour. If the old order feel threatened by new ideas a basic human emotional response system will be activated, the first stage of which is denial. Living with very open frames of reference in the realms of new research and development can be very discomforting, challenging and insecure for some.

Teaching people how to cope with this sort of uncertainty *and* to develop an open outlook is possible. Instead of stress we could help people to develop a sense of excitement over the uncertainty of what might come next.

Many of us are aware that the pace of change is increasing and that we will have to learn to adapt. Also, the trend away from specific divisions of labour within a large structured hierarchy suggests more people will be expected to be involved in increasingly fluid or experimental conditions of work. Matrix and flexible project teams are already commonplace. Someone's discomforting, challenging insecurity is of course someone else's exciting challenge, thrill and enjoyment. To endure the increasing pressure for change we must learn to live with increasing levels of ambiguity.

Ambiguity, multiple domains and 'bubbles'

Many of us have the capacity to play-act, or at least we had the ability as children. Throwing ourselves into a particular role was fun. We could withhold reality long enough to be someone else for a while. Some of us retain this ability as adults, for a variety of different reasons. The behavioural skills are made explicit for actors: both actors and the audience must know how to temporarily suspend belief.

The temporary suspension of belief over what we regard as limitations is one of the most basic requirements of creative thinking. It is possible that a suspension of one set of beliefs in favour of another in our thinking might allow some of us to create separate, sane realities in our minds. This concept might lead us to uncover some useful thinking techniques, for example multiple-domain thinking skills (see box).

Multiple-domain thinking skills

I am indebted to two former girlfriends for the following insight into thinking. At first I took what I was experiencing to be indications of insincerity, but, when the same experience played out on a second occasion some years after the first, I realized there must be a new pattern I had previously missed.

My girlfriend and I were having a really blazing argument. We were both intensely upset, when the phone rang. My mind remained locked and focused on the argument but she answered the telephone. To my amazement, her whole attitude shifted by a quantum leap as she pleasantly acknowledged one of her women friends, promised to call her back, hung up the telephone all sweetness and light, then BOOM! We were back into the argument again!

When this happened a second time with another girlfriend some years later, I realized I had stumbled upon a distinct ability which has something to do with being able to completely separate two ideas and all the associated thoughts that go with them. Perhaps this ability to have two intellectually separate domains in operation at the same time is a skill some men and some women possess.

In my girlfriend's mind, the domain for 'friend' and the one for 'argue' were held quite separately. This is not simply a question of 'rising above' a situation. Clearly this is a useful thinking skill and is possibly related to multitasking abilities. This sort of ability may well have an application in many management practices such as negotiating and managing people with diverse needs. It could also be a way of managing ambiguity and complexity.

During coaching sessions I have noticed some of my clients wanting to keep two domains open when what was actually required in order to move forward was a clear choice of one option over the other. While several of my friends would say they sometimes need to keep their options open, there comes a point when indecision begins to create unnecessary new problems. Perhaps a downside of multitasking ability could be a reluctance to come to decisions in situations where incisive clarity is required. This area of thinking is of interest to me and while I have developed a way of mapping what may be going on, I have not yet devised a way to teach this sort of duality, or twin-track thinking style.

Women *generally* are good at multitasking. Men on the other hand are *generally* not. In *general* men prefer to work on one thing at a time. In biological terms, the cross-connections between the two halves of a typically female brain[2] are far greater in number than in a typically male brain. The female-type brain may be better configured for integrated thought involving multiple domains running concurrently: speech is only processed on one side of the brain in male-type brains while both halves are employed by female-type brains. In the male-type brain the ability to focus may well be a question of more localized brain activity preventing alternative perspectives from surfacing. In male-type brains we might expect the traffic between two opposing halves of the brain to be less, simply because there are fewer neurones connecting each side. Less 'internal communication noise' may enhance focusing ability. In biological terms this may have produced an advantage in creating more focused hunters.

We humans, when compared with other species, are relatively weak animals in the food chain and we need an advantage to survive. Biologically the differences between male-type and female-type brains might be explained in the division of labour. In hunting or fighting it would be more important to be highly focused than to be able to multitask. As we have evolved, the specialization of our brains and of our thinking skills has allowed us to thrive by a combination of being clever *and* being able to co-operate with each other in teams, tribes and nations. Humans are a highly adaptable species. However, we must continue to develop our evolutionary advantage by continuing to learn. A major evolutionary step forward will be to be better able to use all the skills our species naturally possesses. One day it may well be possible for a male-type brain to learn how to emulate multi-domain thinking on demand.

Bubble thinking: A visualization of ambiguity

It may be feasible to achieve holistic thought using a combination of imagery and logic *at the same time*, rather than relying on logic alone to think. Allow yourself the luxury of using a mix of pictures *and* verbal logic when you have to think about complex situations.

Perhaps by being able to visualize the problem as well as to think logically, men may be able to develop an increased faculty to use more parts of their minds and learn how to enjoy ambiguity. Some of the models proposed below may help us to begin to learn how we could keep two conflicting ideas alive and still be able to think clearly. To be viable, two contradictory ideas need to have their own separate spaces in your mind. Bring them too close to each other and they will cancel each other out.

Ambiguity and bubble thinking

Ambiguity usually involves incomplete or contradictory information. Ambiguity can also involve multiple meanings' being attributed to the same words or images. As a consequence a sense of tension is created in our minds. We are aware of the contradictory nature of ambiguous subjects. Part of the contradiction may involve one or more common reference points. In order to resolve the ambiguity, the contradictory thoughts or ideas may fight for the space in our thinking, and either one will come to the fore or they will cancel each other out.

Keeping an open mind

On occasion we may need to keep an open mind, meaning we may need to sustain ambiguous issues in our thinking long enough to resolve other problems. If we want to keep contradictory issues alive in our minds, each idea should exist within some sort of context or separate sub-frame of reference. It may be possible to anchor each of the contradictions to quite separate points within our bigger frames, using logic or imagery, or emotions. In this way it may be possible to hold two contradictory ideas quite separately within a wider frame of reference. Maintaining a degree of openness toward each of the ambiguous ideas requires a sense of trust in oneself.

The ideas can be expressed as equally valid positions, *not* as either/or. It takes an act of will however to maintain two ideas as 'open'.

Ambiguity and bubble thinking

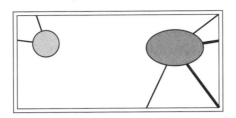

> **Tip** We can be aware of something, but remember – we are not always called upon to comment, judge or decide. Practise withholding a thought or a comment when you feel impelled to make a decision in situations where there is great ambiguity and contradiction. Are you making a decision simply to end the tension or do you want the best decision(s)? Try to find alternative anchors for the opposing ideas and simply refuse to allow yourself to choose for a while.

Ambiguity and choice

In many of my workshops I see managers rushing to choose between options. Ambitious managers seem instinctively compelled to argue with people who disagree. By attacking an opposing view they have reduced their personal tension between the two ideas and have invested greater certainty in one line of thinking in preference to the other. People often miss an easy trick in dealing with two distinctly different ideas. Rather than assume one is right and the other wrong or that one idea is dominant to the other, why not consider *both* as being correct or useful *at the same time*? Multiple solutions can live side by side. A choice or a decision is not always necessary. Sometimes it is valid just to accept what 'is' here and now.

Real advances in individual thinking ability occur when people realize that it *is* acceptable to hold two ideas open at the same time. Even if they are opposites, both ideas could remain true or useful, probably in different ways and with different consequences. In the illustration above, the two conflicting ideas exist inside some sense of reality. Each of the conflicting ideas will have valid connections with established beliefs in a greater, accepted frame of reference.

People often miss an easy trick in dealing with two distinctly different ideas

Ambiguity and the truth

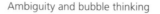

Ambiguity and bubble thinking

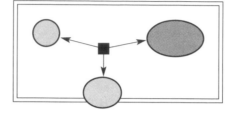

In the illustration above, a variety of potentially contradictory or competing options are viewed from a fixed position. Given the perspective of the person looking at these three possibilities, the lower option will intuitively 'feel' wrong.

The ambiguous information represented by the lowest sphere illustrated above may or may not be a falsehood. Alternatively, what may be at fault is that the perception of the decision maker is too narrow and cannot encompass a big enough frame of reference. Perhaps the difficulty can be overcome by seeking more explanation and/or further exploration. Self-awareness of feelings and intuition will aid the process of mapping roughly where the discomfort exists before an ambiguous option is dismissed out of hand.

> **Tip** A reasonable self-check is to ask yourself, 'Is it me? Am I the problem? Is my perception not big enough to cope with this? Am I being too "square"?' In some circumstances one's own frame of reference may not be big enough to grasp the second person's ideas. Their thinking may literally be too far away from your own. You might choose simply to agree to differ.

New species emerge

Sometimes, to receive the full value of a contradictory bubble of new thoughts or revolutionary ways of doing things, a completely new 'domain' – call it a distinctly new frame of reference – may need to be established. This implies a whole new set of rules, assumptions, experiences and attitudes. In other words, the old frame gives birth to another. (Long gestation periods and

Ambiguity and bubble thinking

birth pains are images that spring to mind here, followed by equally turbulent childhoods and adolescences, including a turbulent leaving-home period.) In business, sometimes the contradiction between two apparently viable yet contradictory options may be too disruptive to hold them in close proximity, and therefore a decision to quash or give the new option complete independence arises. In some cases, organizations bud off new hybrid companies; alternatively individuals leave to set up their own operations, as shown above. Children leave home. Some emigrate.

Sometimes the contradiction between two apparently viable yet contradictory options may be too disruptive to hold them in close proximity

Viewed dispassionately, the process of separation between groups of people with two vastly different outlooks may be analyzed rationally but, among those who are directly involved, passions about the right course of action will run high. To those who stay in the old paradigm, the change will feel highly illogical: their perception will be that people they were previously close to have suddenly developed a mad idea and set off on an equally insane journey, to an uncertain future. By contrast, for the people leaving, the thrill of the unknown and a pioneer spirit will be both appealing and invigorating!

Bubble thinking or insincerity?

Lies and ambiguity

There are degrees of ambiguity, and then there is obfuscation (i.e. fog and fudge), and then there are lies. When dealing with ambiguous information, a person may genuinely believe the separate domains to be honest and true, but they may be unwittingly shielding themselves for some reason: for

> **Tip** There is a danger in displaying an ability to move between vastly different domains of thinking without showing a judgement. Such a person may appear either manipulative or insincere. Care is therefore needed in the display of such a skill. If someone else's frame of reference is closed to you, then explaining how they might be able to reframe or deal with the inherent contradictions and how both might remain viable under different circumstances may not always be welcome. You may be mobile in your own thinking; the other person may not be. In any event it is always better to hold your own counsel until asked.

example, denial may be at work. Ambiguity and convincing lies have some common ground. Both are often incomplete and both have some basis in true facts. One way to disguise a lie is to give the lie a foundation in truth.

When thinking about great ambiguities and huge uncertainties, care is required in testing one's own understanding and basic assumptions before any judgement of the truth is attempted.

Ambiguity and bubble thinking

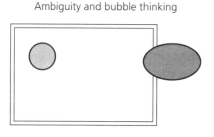

> **Tip** I have suggested a whole series of images of ambiguity that work for me. What works for you? If you can begin to develop your own visual metaphors for ambiguity as we go through the book, then the concepts we build up can work better for you.

In summary

Learning to live with ambiguity requires a sense of humour. Why? Well, one needs to be able to feel comfortable at the edge of uncertainty where the boundaries are non-existent or elastic. This particular edge is an un reasonable place to be. Most senior directors and leading-edge artists will recognize this place. At such a place there are stark choices, which are all emotional – you either laugh or you get angry or despair. One attitude leads to a fun, playful approach whereas ultimately the other leads to seriousness and assertive control as a way of dealing with uncertainty.

Living or thinking at the edge, where ambiguity is rife, demands huge amounts of mental energy because our thinking boundaries are constantly being challenged. Some will find this invigorating while others will shy away drained, after brief sorties. At least if you possess a map of the territory you stand a better chance of staying sane (and, if you are an artist, of keeping both your ears).

Dealing with ambiguity will become a core skill for most managers in the future as markets globalize, fragment and speed up. In this chapter there are a variety of ideas and images that may help you think through ambiguous situations. You may find the image of Yin–Yang or the splits or the bubble concept useful.

If you can think using words *and* at the same time use imagery to visualize the ambiguity, you may engage more mental muscle in resolving your dilemmas. If you fail to resolve an ambiguity, I hope you will learn to find the humour in it.

The trouble with ambiguity is that, while it can cause great amusement, ambiguous information renders the truth elusive and difficult to pin down. If you are about to make major life or strategic business decisions, being able to deal with this sort of information will be important. With this in mind, the next chapter looks at how we might manage our expectations and interpretation of 'the truth'.

Notes

1 Source: *Polarity Management*™ by Barry Johnson. Copyright 1992, 1996. Published by HRD Press, Inc., Amherst, Massachusetts, 800–822–2810, www.hrdpress.com.

2 Apparently scientists can, by a sound test, relatively easily differentiate between a typically male brain and a typically female brain, irrespective of actual gender. No inference on sexual preferences can be made or is intended by this division: some women have a typically male brain and some men have a typically female brain. Psychologists and scientists are looking principally at patterns of thinking in the majority of males and females.

The truth and expectations

9

Incomplete information can lead to ambiguity. One of the most difficult things to think about is the truth and what constitutes reasonable expectations; this is especially so in ambiguous situations. Business life and our personal lives are full of grey areas out of which we need to try to form reasonable decisions or develop a plan of action. Deciding upon a course to set for the future of a business, with so many grey areas to deal with, is just as difficult as planning for your own lifetime. So how do we determine what is true or reasonable? What kind of maps can we develop to help us work smarter?

In an absolute world, where all answers are clear cut and devoid of ambiguity, the absolute truth, the correct answer, should be easy to find. Life is not like that, though. The price we pay for the rich variety we experience is increasing ambiguity. In business life, lots of the really big issues involve degrees of ambiguity. In a complex, fast-moving world the truth can be difficult to find. The right answer may be a question of context, opinion or interpretation. If the answer to a question is 'It depends', then we would want to know, 'On what?'

When thinking about 'grey-scale' truths, I find that graph shapes help create a guiding context. Rather than defining places, graphs can convey a sense of flow. In this chapter we will look at how we can use a variety of relatively simple graph shapes to guide our thinking.

Truth and transition: Curves, waves and beliefs

Graphs and waves are really useful thinking tools. This is because they are *generally* familiar shapes: we do not usually have to explain the basic notions behind what 'a graph' is. By contrast, if we were to start to explain something using an image such as a tree, we would have to begin by explaining why we chose a particular tree and why using an illustration of a tree might help before we got into the substance of the reasoning.

Graphs exist in our common reasoning as a tool in science and in business. However, not everyone uses them beyond explaining how a pattern of numbers might behave. Roughly drawn graph shapes can be used without numbers to help us think about and more clearly visualize complex transition events in our lives.

In this chapter we will look at how we can interpret situations using the fundamental characteristics of two differently shaped curves. If we can understand the basic 'shape of a situation' by using these curves, then perhaps we can assess and react in a better way. First we shall look at what statisticians describe as a 'normal distribution curve', which has a bell shape.

How it is

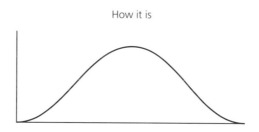

These can be used to represent the continuum of static situations.

The second simple shape we will consider is a 'sine wave', which undulates like a snake. This sort of wave has a regular pattern. It is a sort of 'what goes around comes around' shape. This sort of shape can be useful where we seem to encounter repeating situations. The rhythm of these snake-like sine wave curves may be long and slow, while at other times the shape may change much more quickly. A sine wave can suggest movement within a fixed frame or it can present the richer image of a snake choosing to move where it will, without boundaries.

Bell curves

How scientists use a bell curve

This sort of chart is used by mathematicians, biologists and all sorts of scientists to see if an event is a chance occurrence or something genuinely different from what might be normally expected. A bell curve indicates that the incidence of things is evenly distributed. The scientists call them normal distribution curves. This sort of curve has a beginning and an end. Usually the vertical scale of the graph represents the number or incidence of whatever we measure; the horizontal scale is a measure of the feature that we are interested in. (But when using the bell curve as a thinking tool, we are interested more in the general shape and the use we can put it to in our minds without using numbers.)

A typical bell-shaped, normal distribution occurs because within very large samples there is an even spread of both usual *and* unusual events that could occur randomly, by chance. The calculations associated with tracking unusual events look at the probability of their happening by chance. The lower the probability the event is due to chance, the higher the odds are that a cluster of unusual events is *not* a random, natural event but is actually indeed unique. The unusual events are usually in the thin 'tails' of the chart because fewer natural occurrences are found there. For example, if we were to measure population height, the horizontal axis would be marked off in measures of height from left to right. The vertical axis would be marked off in thousands or millions depending on how many people we chose to take as a sample. Very few people are really small (left-hand 'tail' of the graph) and very few people are very tall (right-hand tail of the graph); most people fall in the middle zone. Significantly different events, therefore, are those that are not so common and will be found at the two ends, the two 'tails' of the graph. What occurs in the middle is usual: there is lots of it and it can therefore be predicted.

Using our example of the height survey, we might expect we would normally encounter three giants or four really tiny adults in the sample. If we found 20, then we would know that something unusual was happening.

▶

Should we repeat the height survey in different places, the graphs would be likely to be the same shape but slightly higher or lower up the scale, depending which country one chose to do the survey in. For example, *in general* people are taller in Scandinavia than in Bangladesh. We can see that a tall person in one country may be regarded as only average in another. What is normal in one domain becomes unusual in another. So the answer to the question 'Are you tall?' is 'It depends on who I am compared with'. Graphs drawn for each country might be the same shape but simply use different scales. So the truth about being tall becomes a relative truth. I am generally considered tall in England but of only average height when stood alongside Scandinavian men.

Let's begin by looking at how we might use a bell curve for thinking about 'the truth' or for finding answers to complex subjects in business and in our relationships. A distribution curve is described as normal if the shape is evenly balanced. Most events fit in the middle and the unusual happenings occur at the two edges, or the 'tails', as these ends of the curve are sometimes called. Not all situations are evenly spread, though. Sometimes the bell curve may be pushed to the left or to the right of centre by some kind of bias. Distribution is then 'skewed', one way or the other.

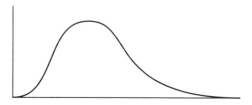

When a skewed distribution occurs, what is considered 'normal' within the sample is skewed away from what might have been expected within an even distribution. Take wealth distribution as an example. The curve for wealth distribution could be evenly spread in some countries under a normal distribution curve while in others the shape of the curve may be heavily skewed towards poverty.

Use of the shape

We can imagine a crudely drawn shape in our minds and, without attributing numbers, estimate the position within the curve of information we receive. All of these curves might help us to crudely classify events within some sort of overall contextual shape. For example, a man who owns $10,000 might be regarded as relatively rich in a very poor country whereas he would be unexceptional in the USA. In a poor country he is at one end of the scale and at the opposite end in a richer country. In other words, these are devices that help us to position information within a relative context. Mathematicians use this sort of information to tell them to pay attention to something when it does not fit the usual pattern. Cold facts, such as owning $10,000, mean nothing until they are put into the right kind of context.

These shapes tell us where information 'sits' relative to other similar information and this can help our interpretation of a good answer relative to a bad one, within a context. Using these bell shapes can help us to interpret complex issues in daily life and to form the information into a relative pattern. When information is placed in the proper context, it becomes less difficult to think about our judgements and decisions. If we also understand the total cluster of information and the shape it makes, we are in a better position to think about unusual situations within the cluster. We can then do what our minds are best arranged for – we can manage by exception.

Bell curves and absolute or relative truth

Earlier in the book we noted that some problems can be considered clear cut while many are not. Our interpretation of 'truth' can also be clear cut or relative. This is an important distinction to make, since many people put a high emotional investment into a particular truth without first understanding whether the truth is absolute or partial. In considering the relative position of truth we can also put our expectations into an appropriate context. Being either 'right' or 'wrong' may depend upon a particular context or the interpretation at a given time. Under these circumstances truth becomes *relative*.

Many people put a high emotional investment into a particular truth without first understanding whether the truth is absolute or partial

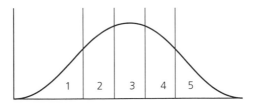

Taking the idea of 'truth' or absolute right and wrong, we could use a bell curve model to put perceptions of truth into compartments and look at truth in a relative way. In the illustration above, I have divided the curve into five zones. This picture attempts to capture 'grey areas of truth'. The following example illustrates how there may be a clash between simplistic logic and relative issues by contrasting what happens in Zone 5 relative to Zone 1.

Consider the question of business entertaining. At what point does entertaining a business guest become a temptation to sway judgement or even a crude bribe? A wealthy person takes an employee of another organization to lunch. Both are very busy and working over lunch is seen as an efficient use of time by both. So far, so good. However, a meal can cost £10, £30, £50, £80, £120, £150 or £250; excluding wine or tax. The meeting is a business meeting and we should be aware that the employee is able to trade with the host; so at what level would one decide that the level of entertaining is inappropriate? The answer is 'It depends'. For instance if the client being entertained was the governor of the Bank of England and the host the Sultan of Brunei, a Zone 5 situation, the guest might be offended if lunch was a hamburger and a coke, which would be more appropriate in Zone 1. On the other hand a buyer from a small company would consider a bill of £150 excessive.

So where would you call the limit on 'reasonable entertainment expenses'? The answer may be obvious within your own context, less so in some other domain. Using the bell curve reminds us of relativity. What is normal for people in Zone 5 will be excessive for those in Zone 1.

To illustrate the point further, in a 1998 court case a UK judge ruled that a claim for $50,000 was excessive for the redecoration of the walls of five rooms that had been allegedly spoiled by a tenant. The judge cut the award for Lady X to only $30,000! Clearly we are in Zone 5 here!

The truth and legal conflict

What actually constitutes 'the truth' is very much a matter of interpretation because so few things in life are absolute. For this reason, anyone going to prove a point in a court of law should abandon at the door all their hopes and expectations, however rational these may seem. Even if we believe we have the truth on our side, when we go to court we are asking others to interpret our reality. What you think and believe to be 'the truth' can ultimately become a question of money. This is because the most money often buys the most agile, quality minds who are able to shape the relevant information so that it is seen as the truth in the eyes of those making the final judgment.

Anyone going to prove a point in a court of law should abandon at the door all their hopes and expectations

Exercise 1

Bell curves can be used to profile your business. If you are marketing a product or service, who are your customers and where within a bell shape are the various groups distributed? What segments can be identified? Within these segments, which customers would be most valued by someone else? Alternatively you might consider the age distribution of current customers. Is the curve you choose a normal curve?

Add time to the thought process and crudely estimate how the customer profile will change if you decide not to recruit new customers. Will your product offering remain relevant to the existing ones as they age?

Think now about your organization. If we drew the curves for the following measures, which ones would suddenly have strategic importance?

- What is the age distribution of my employees?
- Is this uniform throughout the company?
- What is the distribution of our worldwide business in terms of age, nationality, sex, aspirations and social styles?
- Do these curves match the composition of our middle management and of the board of directors?

In other words, do the shapes of your company profile match those of your customers? If not, how can you expect to think like them?

Sine waves

A sine wave looks like a letter 'S' on its side. It's curvy and continuous. One major characteristic of a sine wave is that it represents a continuum. A sine wave can be another way of drawing a circle in a linear way. In other words, a sine wave suggests 'What goes around comes around!' I like to think of these images as fast or slow snakes. The fast ones you can usually see or hear but the slow ones can be just as deadly: they creep up and catch you unawares!

Wave forms

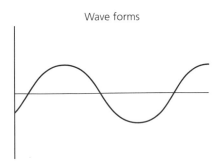

The bigger the boom, the longer the bust; someone has to pay

Situations and experiences will tend to repeat until something truly fundamental changes the cycle. Snake waves can be used for thinking about the patterns of events. The trick is to recognize the frequency at which things come around again. The trouble with long waves is we forget earlier pattern events or we fail to see the trend because it is so insidiously slow. Recession always, *always* follows boom. The bigger the boom, the longer the bust; someone has to pay. Sine waves can help us think about the behaviour of events over the longer term, revealing both problems and opportunities.

Personal waves

Wave forms can be used to help us understand our personal lives too: for example there may be a natural rhythm to the way our bodies and minds work. We may work best at certain times and need rest specifically at others. When your rhythm is in step with someone else's there might be a harmony.

Disharmony may simply be a question of being out of step with your own or other people's rhythms. The rhythm might be energy, stage in life, hormonal state (for men and women) or our emotional, spiritual, sexual or financial needs. Our needs are not static – they rise and fall like a barometer over time. Do you know what your own needs are and how they rise and fall? Have you ever tried to plot them?

Our relationships may follow wave patterns. In our most personal relationships, being in love does not always mean being in harmony. Being out of step with the rhythms of one's partner may not necessarily mean being out of love with one another either. It is possible that 'love' exists in waves and is more available or less available to our partners depending on how much energy or compassion we are able to offer at any particular time. 'Lucky in love' might mean knowing how to make your waves or rhythms move in harmony with those of your partner for more of the time. The course of true love never runs straight. We should learn to accept that there will be low points that need to be worked on, times for resolving differences, forgiving mistakes, growing and moving on up again.

The nature of love itself may change too. It may not be comfortable to stay with someone you love when you are both frequently out of phase. This 'out of phase' is like being 'in love deferred'. All the correct feelings may be there, but simply out of alignment at that moment.

If you can think through and adopt these principles in your personal life then by analogy you should be able to employ the same lessons in business. Working out the rules of life is always difficult because we are not born with the manual or the rulebook. Even if we were given such godly gifts, someone else would rewrite both the rules and the manual just to make life more interesting! The central observation, therefore, is that we must remain alert and aware of the pattern of our lives, both at home and at work, and be ready to adapt. In order to be effective players, though, we need to formulate our own big picture and to try to work out our own rules. The graphs produced by the two exercises later in this chapter aim to produce just such a big picture.

Complex waves

There are many free and simple pleasures in life, such as enjoying the sight of young animals or children at play, a warm harmonious sunset or fresh flowers in bloom. The joy in the act of looking is simple, yet much of life appears intricate, both in our jobs and in our personal lives. These apparently complicated issues seem to absorb most of our time. The complexity of the path of our lives might be seen as a tangled web. Many of the forces that we experience in our lives do have a pattern that, once understood, helps us understand and accommodate what is happening. We can attempt to understand some of what is going on by visualizing the patterns using short- and long-wave imagery. By gaining an understanding of these wave-like patterns, we can begin to see how and when they might affect us. We can see high and low points and therefore better prepare ourselves to choose how and when to react. (I am particularly grateful to Graham Rawlinson for introducing me to this particular thinking tool.)

Multiple wave forms

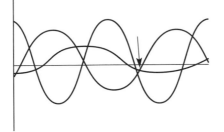

A simple place to start is to plot a series of trends

If we were able to discover what forces were acting upon us, we might end up with a graph such as the one above. This illustration shows a composite wave forming. Note that all three trends take a dive at one point below the line. This might seem like a period of hard luck at the time, but if such a time could be foreseen, perceptions of personal pressure could be forestalled. Looking at events in isolation distracts from the big picture and can undermine the quality of your thinking.

If we live only from moment to moment we may enjoy summer but freeze in winter.

Do you have an image of what your big picture looks like at work or in your personal life? For some people it's a fog, others might see a collage of imagery, while some may see lists and routines. Some people may have a variety of models. It may be that for many people their big picture is vague or simply not something they care to think about. A simple place to start is to plot a series of trends.

We can start by trying to identify the forces that might affect you. See Exercises 2 and 3 below. In both cases the trick is first to identify the forces and *not* to view them in isolation. Map them all out on one large chart so that you can see how they interact and how they accumulate or decline together. Throw in major change points and see what coincides. In doing this exercise it may be wise to choose the most important forces and map these in different combinations. The precise times and amounts do not matter. This is a rough exercise that can highlight how a variety of events or forces combine to help or hinder.

This format works just as much in the workplace as it does in one's personal life. It can be a crude measuring stick, but it will alert you to major weak points or opportunities in the future.

In order to get to grips with the major forces at work on one's personal life, several attempts to develop a useful and relevant map may be needed. Timescales may be rough and vague, but they will generally give an indication as to approximately when the good and the bad times are likely to occur in our lives. For example: we all retire; children grow up and go to college; we may get married, get divorced, be made redundant and take retraining; our parents get ill and die; job success ebbs and flows. There are also certain trends that affect us all, for example: personal energy is likely to be higher at 30 than at 50, we are more at risk as we age, financial earning-growth peaks at a given point and starts to fall as we grow older, our living costs go up and down dramatically – the list goes on and on. In business, new technologies appear, whole industries are moved to lower-cost countries, new competitors emerge, profit margins erode, employee availability and co-operation change, the level of government intervention changes, staff and customers age, the price of fuel and assets goes up and down, things that were plentiful become scarce, high-value items become generic commodities, and phoenixes rise from the ashes reinvigorated.

Once you appreciate the influence of steady change, try the exercises below. The questions may not be the best for you: they are simply to get you into the idea of doing this exercise. Try finding the important questions in your life or in your business and customizing the charts to match your needs and interests.

Exercise 2: Business complex waves

List the sort of things that can affect your business or your industry over the next 5 to 20 years, for example:

- company energy level (e.g. average staff ages: 25 vs 35 vs 45 vs 55)
- quality of staff
- natural business cycle
- global business cycle
- workload
- finance in/out
- debt load
- new business additions/consequent work load/ finance flow
- business disposals
- new forces
- new technology
- customer changes, e.g. age, aspirations, needs, etc.
- supplier changes
- raw material.

List another ten issues/events/processes in the next 5 to 20 years:

1 _____

2 _____

3 _____

4 _____

5 _____

6 _____

7 _____

8 _____

9 _____

10 _____

Now roughly plot all your most important patterns on the same chart.

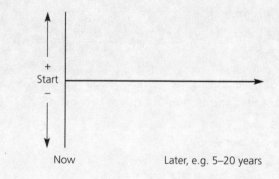

Having created a map, interpret the places where there appear to be lots of lines intersecting or where there are extreme highs or lows. Look also for times where things appear to collide or be in sequence. Where will you need bolstering and where will you be at an advantage?

Exercise 3: Personal complex waves

List the sort of things in your personal life that can affect you over a long period of time, for example:

- personal energy level
- natural circadian rhythm
- workload
- finance in/out
- family additions
- bereavements.

List another ten events or processes in the next 5 to 20 years:

1 _____

2 _____

3 _____

4 _____

5 _____

6 _____

7 _____

8 _____

9 _____

10 _____

Now roughly plot all your most important patterns on the same chart.

Having created a map, interpret the places where there appear to be lots of lines intersecting, or where there are extremes, or where things appear to collide or be in sequence. Where will you need bolstering and where will you be at an advantage?

▶

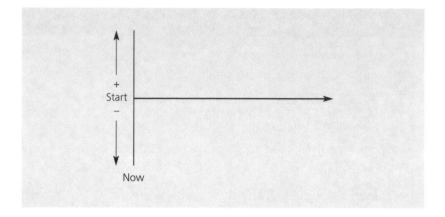

In summary

In this chapter we looked at bell curves and sine waves, or 'snake-like graphs', which can be used to make a clear image of a complex issue. The bell curve can help us think through relative positions of information within a belief system. The sine wave and other free-form waves make it possible to draw a composite picture of a variety of forces that operate in sequence over a long period of time. Compiling a composite wave chart can help us see the big picture in our lives as well as in our business and prepare us for the roller-coaster ride of life.

These curves and lines are all simple, yet in combination with other forms can illuminate our perception of our work, of our future possibilities and of our personal development. Graph shapes may be used to help us think about the dynamic aspects of our life and to see how these *flow* relative to other aspects. Real life is rarely static, absolute or pure. Nature seems to like it that way.

Now that we have moved from ambiguity to an examination of how we might think about relative truths, the next chapter will look at how we might deal with totally unstructured information using maps of 'contexts'.

Radar and the big picture: Context

10

As busy professionals, we are often faced with complicated situations where we are not sure what is going on; occasionally we might lack confidence in our ability to adequately think through and deal with what life throws at us. Complicated situations are often made easier to understand if we first consider the shape and form of the context. In this chapter we will think about context, horizons and how big your 'radar screen' is.

When we are able to visualize the wider context of our lives, to recognize where our boundaries are and where we fit within the wider scheme of things, it becomes possible to develop the choices we need to lead a productive life. The following thinking tools are based upon images that can help us shape our thoughts about context.

Contexts are internal and external

Few things exist in a total void. Things and thoughts exist relative to one another.

Often we are aware of the importance of relating to each other, but we may miss the importance of our relationship within the context in which we are operating. A context can have a material impact upon the way that we think and choose to act. Therefore it is worth thinking specifically about our context and how our immediate environment might shape our thinking and decision making, the people we spend most time with and where we most frequently place our mind's attention.

Our thinking may be shaped by what we expose our attention to, wittingly or subconsciously. The clothes we wear and the places we occupy shape us as much as we shape them. Do the shoes break you in or you them? When you live in a neighbourhood, do you shape it or does it shape you? Old proverbs such as 'You can judge a person by the company they keep' are simplistic examples of established wisdom that understands that other people affect the way individuals think and behave. If you spend all of your working life as a prison warder, do you become the longest-serving prisoner? The people you choose to spend your time with, your physical environment and your commercial, aesthetic and spiritual climate will, in the long run, influence the way you think.

> **Tip** In considering your personal context, reflect upon who you spend time with and why. How rich is your social life? Are you even slightly influenced by other factors? What are these? Who might help you pin them down? They might include your surroundings, the clothes you wear, your spiritual associations, your beliefs and your values. If you changed any of the above in order to feel better in yourself, which changes would have the most valuable effect upon you and why?

Our internal map of the world evolves as we live and think, but it is rare for someone to sit down and draw it out on paper. By knowing the map's features, we can understand the subtle forces that shape us. Creating a map of our context can inform us where and what the signposts are and help us navigate to a better place. Alternatively, context maps can aid us in making more of where we are now.

Our thinking about situations can sometimes be unnecessarily narrow.

All the world is a stage on which we play and we must not forget that the scenery does, in good plays, change reasonably frequently

Occasionally our mental map of the world may become too narrowly focused, for example upon the next big job, a business issue, a person or a thing, without taking into account the 'big picture'. When we focus, we lose sight of the surrounding detail, the incidentals and the scenery around us. All the world is a stage on which we play and we must not forget that the scenery does, in good plays, change reasonably frequently. In some situations the changes in our lives may be dramatic and visible, while on other occasions they are so gradual and slow as to be imperceptible. If we miss the scenery changing, we will be unaware that our assumptions, decisions and behaviour may become inappropriate. We should pay attention to the scenery, to the bigger picture of our personal and work lives, because the way we think and behave can be profoundly influenced by it.

> **Tip** Make sure that each day you pay close attention to something pleasant but trivial that you would not otherwise give your attention to. Two minutes a day will make a difference, especially if you maintain a brief, cumulative written record of what you have enjoyed in these observations.

> **Tip** Many people associate 'big picture' with their life's purpose and journey. One way of getting a lifelong perspective on the context of your life is to imagine being handed a plaque inscribed with your life's biggest achievements, those for which other meaningful people would thank you. Imagine exactly what the plaque would say now and at two future points in time. Who would hand you the plaque and who would be your audience?

Tools for visualizing contexts

In order to think about the wider context for thinking, I like to use a combination of concepts. These include three-dimensional space, radar and boundaries. Images that can help us visualize such concepts include a variety of shapes such as a bubble, an onion, or perhaps an egg shape or, if you think you can handle it, you might even choose a 3D box-frame of reference.

Holistic thinking

As an amateur artist, I notice that there is beauty in symmetry; however, I also notice that asymmetrical objects hold their own attractions. With this in mind we will first use an egg as a 3D image to help us think relatively about context and later in this chapter we will employ the shape of an onion. Each of these shapes has the characteristics of an inner space, an outside and edges.

Whatever shape is chosen, it should enclose the wider perceived reality: within it exists all of the issue, the problem or the opportunity. The outer boundary may be the edge of our awareness or the edge of the current frame of reference that we believe to be true.

Context and thinking

In this simple example, an egg shape represents the bigger context into which you fit; you and your thoughts and perceptions are all positioned somewhere inside. Life is dynamic, alive, so again in this model neither the bigger picture nor the subjects are fixed and both are free to move independently of each other.

Boundaries can move

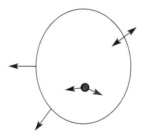

Feeling lucky?

In this model, let's assume that solving a problem or getting what you want means the inner circle making contact with the edge of the bigger shape. If one adopts a static position, 'good luck' may be the movement of the bigger picture towards you, in your favour. In effect, what you want just happens to be moving in your direction.

Context and 'luck'

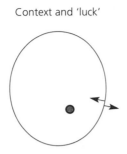

Bad luck would be the opposite. Stand still long enough and you will experience both! Luck in this instance is therefore a question of being in the right place at the right time. I do believe people can be lucky, but I don't believe we are meant to passively place all our bets on luck alone. If your thinking and decision process is predisposed to 'depend on luck', you might consider changing your perspective.

The more ground you cover, the higher the likelihood that you will understand your life well. It also appears likely that the more active a person is, the higher their chance of getting a result, depicted in this model as making contact with the edge. Frenetic activity may mean more errors, but also a higher chance of getting a result.

If we adopt a determined strategy to understand the bigger picture and the way it moves, then we can see how it becomes possible to position ourselves better, so that good 'luck' occurs by design and not by chance. To do that we have to open our eyes and minds and become sensitive to the wider context within which we live and operate. Once we are lucky by design, the almost superstitious view of luck may be replaced by a more positive view of self-determination and of personal success.

Tip If you believe your life is mostly a question of good or bad luck, reconsider what forces are at work in your life. Ask yourself how they affect the way you choose to think and what you think under the influence of these other forces. Remember you have a choice over which thoughts you pay attention to. Widen your focus so you can see the bigger picture, then narrow your focus on to those things you can have an impact upon. Don't be put off if you are only able to have partial influence on an outcome. Sometimes starting up a partial result leads to a bigger than expected impact.

Other people as context

Life is complex. Whether we like it or not, we share our personal worlds with other people. Life is especially complicated when we have responsibility for other people.

We are not alone

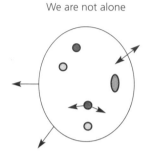

When we are faced with complexity we may sometimes misjudge the importance of other people within the context. We may overestimate their importance and influence. Alternatively we may be aware of their presence but we may forget they are available to help. For example, how often have you been surprised by who actually turned out to help you when you really needed assistance in a crisis? Who let you down is usually an even bigger surprise. We tend not to pay enough attention to the contexts we are in and to the shifting nature of the strength of our relationships. As time passes, not all of us pay conscious attention to how boundaries and the quality of relationships shift.

> **Tip** When thinking about complex situations, it is worthwhile trying to draw a crude map of what the whole situation is about. Attempt to define approximately where the boundaries are now, where they are likely to move to and by when. Then check 'where' in the scheme of things other people 'fit'. Try to discover what their main interests and relationships to each other and to the situation are. People's tenure of influence wears out just like car tyres. How will the passage of time change your big picture and your relationships within it?

Control versus collaboration

One of our responses to complexity is to get 'organized'. We do this in our minds first. The problem with our thinking, though, is that as adults we employ previous experience and prior belief patterns. These are embedded in our frames of reference. We begin with a pattern of beliefs that shape the way we think and behave. Thus, before we even engage conscious thinking, we may already be subconsciously predisposed to a particular pattern of thought. The difference between the philosophies of control and collaboration illustrates this.

As managers mature, some learn that the concept of possessing 'power and control' is actually nothing more than a temporary illusion. Most meaningful endeavours, they discover, are successful when people's hands, hearts and minds collaborate.

There are situations where it is possible to achieve a clear sense of control. In a crisis, for example, people seem predisposed to align behind a leader and may 'for the good of the many' permit themselves to be controlled, until the crisis passes. Taking control in business by remaining in a constant state of crisis is not really a viable long-term option. Intelligent people enjoy a sense of direction and of being led, yet at the same time they give their best when they are able to collaborate. Too much control turns people off. Great leaders need great followers, who follow by consent.

> **Taking control in business by remaining in a constant state of crisis is not really a viable long-term option**

Despite this, some managers think that 'control' is the answer to complex contexts when what is actually needed is collaboration. Unfortunately people fail to learn about the illusion of power and the need to think in terms of collaboration rather than control. They spend their lives in frustration complaining, unsurprisingly, that they cannot get things done.

Tip It is important to think through *how* you are going to achieve what needs to be done in an organization. I would suggest you develop a series of your own image models that will help you 'see' how you can influence other people. Part of your model toolbox should include images of context, other participants and a variety of boundaries.

Thinking about context and control: Climbing the career ladder

Continuing with the thinking about control, there is a basic fault in the logic that when a person arrives at the top of a big organization they will have full control and feel fulfilled, safe or perhaps happier. This sort of aspiration is rarely fulfilled. The bigger the context, the less likely that any one person will have full control. When managers reach the top, they find that they have reached the edge where the levers of power exist but the centre of their world is now hollow! Between top-level power and front-line implementation is a void. Collaboration is still required. Even when a director reaches the top, there are still yet more people in new contexts who will or will not comply with their needs, such as shareholders, the media, pressure groups, unions, government, and so on. Each of these constituents has their own 'worlds' and their own bigger contexts to satisfy. Full control remains elusive. In effect we are all middle managers. The majority of us are at least in the middle between our organization and our customers. We rarely have long-term control over our customers. If you think you *do* control your customers then think again: if you have this mindset they are no longer customers but hostages and that is a whole other story.

Reached the top and still
not in control!

No matter how big you get, there is always a bigger context within which you fit. Being in 'control' of a situation is an illusion. Once we realize this explicitly, our thinking can be more productively directed to produce the most effective impact with issues or people, where we can have an influence.

Effectiveness is a matter of balancing your energy output to produce the maximum impact. As a manager, any attempt to do everything and control *all* things will simply demand too much energy and time. The result is poor collective performance and, not surprisingly, ill health.

The way you think can clearly affect your health. Harder work is not the answer as you get promoted. It's more a matter of intelligence and stamina, and of thinking and behaving in a smarter way.

In all matters beyond simple decisions, thinking will be a matter of balancing the different priorities of different parts of the wider context. In any organization there are usually not enough resources to pursue all the ambitions of all the people. Balancing a variety of competing interests can be complicated. Unfortunately decisions involving any level of complexity can easily become political. If you are uncomfortable with thinking about or dealing with politics, then this is an area you will need to improve if you want to aspire to higher management positions. If you do find yourself involved in something political, try to separate emotion from transaction and, wherever possible, do the right thing for as many people as you can.

A top managerial position requires a different approach to thinking from that needed by someone in a more junior position. If managers and leaders fail to see the widest possible context, they could miss significant opportunities or fall foul of a bigger force that had been overlooked.

> **If you find yourself involved in something political, try to separate emotion from transaction and, wherever possible, do the right thing for as many people as you can**

Tip If you are seeking promotion to a more senior position, be aware of the different expectations of your new peer group in regard to your ability to think, to reflect and to offer well-thought-through, balanced ideas.

Scanning for the big picture and seeing the game in play

As management structures fragment or are flattened, the number of people who become responsible for the long-term success of an organization increases. Clearly this is risky if this larger body of people lack the time, inclination or skills to think about the future. So if your career is likely to involve clear responsibility for planning for the future, then being able to 'scan' widely for information to fuel your thoughts is very important, all the more so the higher up an organization you rise. Even experienced thinkers can fail to see the bigger picture, especially if a chord is struck that is too close to home.

Scanning is not simply a question of gathering facts or snippets of fragmented information. It is absolutely essential not only to have a wide awareness of the territory but also, given the political atmosphere of many environments where complex decisions are made, to be able to see the motives of others for what they really are. Not everyone is there to help. So in thinking about planning, we need to scan widely for information of a soft as well as a hard kind: people's motivations, feelings, expectations and individual needs. Politics can be just as deadly as a bullet. Other people's political intentions need to be raised in your mind, made explicit and mapped.

Networking and mentoring

There are two *very* important behaviours that aid thinking in wide, complex contexts. First, if you want to be informed and intellectually challenged by others, it is vital to have the ability to network, both internally and, in particular, externally.

> **Tip** Review your attitude to networking. Do you do enough? Is your network wide enough to give you a good span of input and diverse enough to sufficiently challenge the content, scope and quality of what you think?

The second important behaviour is mentoring. This meets both the networking and the altruistic needs of top-level managers and directors. When all around are offering politically biased views of reality, a younger manager can be a rich source of information about what is *really* going on in the organization. This can be immensely valuable to a director in helping shape his or her thinking about future decisions. For a variety of reasons senior managers often find themselves isolated from what is really going on and it can be quite lonely at the top too. A conversation with a younger person can be invigorating and refreshing.

In return an older manager can offer wise advice on how to think through complex or controversial decisions. Also, importantly, a mentor may possess the power or the contacts to implement a younger manager's idea.

> **Tip** Do you have a mentor? If the answer is 'No', go get one, informally. Seek the advice of a senior manager you like and then ask for permission to return. It is important that you do not overplay the opportunity to contact your mentor. Ideally a mentor should be in a position of authority, but removed from your immediate line of managers. Try to remain open and respectful and to keep any confidences that are shared with you. Over your career you will have more than one mentor. If you look back, you may realize you have already had more than one mentor in your life. Is someone benevolently watching over you now?

Acting as a mentor can make you feel revitalized and closer to the action. Young people's enthusiasm is a great antidote to dusty old cynicism. Mentoring can also help you to find out what the 'troops' actually think or what is really going on in the business. Occasionally you may need to protect your apprentices from others and from themselves. Where possible the latter is best done prospectively.

> **Tip** If you are a director, ask yourself when was the last time you made a space in your diary to spend time helping and guiding a younger manager you liked? Perhaps you can have fun by proxy by developing the career of someone young whom you admire.

Building your own models

Logic cross

Ever wondered why consultants love creating logic crosses? It's the simplest way of creating a sense of relativity. Sailors, pilots or anyone trying to find their way across wide-open, featureless seas have used maps for centuries. When we look for a place on a map we use grid references. Two points crossed over tell us where we are *relative* to other places. A piece of information is difficult to place if it is not relative to something else.

Almost everything exists relative to something else. A vague idea or a nebulous piece of information becomes easier to deal with if we can fix it relative to something else. So, if you need a simple model, start by crossing two factors to see what you get. For example, if we attach a high and low value to 'service needs' and 'customer loyalty' we get:

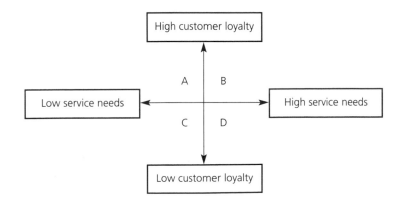

This sort of cross produces a minimum of four spaces that can be more clearly defined by their extremes. In the example above it becomes possible to classify four quite different types of customer, A, B, C and D, using these two unusual metrics.

Pairing and contrasting different high-impact uncertainties is the basic technique for reducing uncertainty and for modelling possible futures or 'scenarios'.

Try analogy

Gardening analogies can be quite powerful

Alternatively, if you prefer something more abstract to use to build your own models, try thinking a little more creatively (see also Chapter 11). A map or a model is simply a representation that helps us with a real situation. In the same way as we use an object such as a map to help us, we can use other everyday abstractions to help us think. One very common abstraction is our ability to think in terms of analogies.

Analogies can fuel simple imagery. Try it. For example, here's a simple gardening analogy: 'Rooting out corruption is like trying to remove stinging nettles. The plants fight back and if the gardener leaves behind even the smallest root, up they spring again.' Gardening analogies can be quite powerful.

As a second example of an analogy, try this: if you had to give a situation the character of a person, whom would you choose and what would their age be, etc.?

Once you have your analogy, use what the image represents and the richness of implied meaning that goes with it. Pursue the imagery for as long as possible to suggest meaning or lessons.

Strategic frontiers

The quality of what we think is influenced by the way we model the world within our perception and by the information we accept into our minds. We may receive information, but our minds may not necessarily accept it.

Having diverse people stretch our intellectual boundaries is one way of staying mentally fresh. Even the best network and mentors in the world will only take you so far.

The furthest frontier is being able to think about complex situations where the information is diffuse, fragmented or very much open to inter-pretation and incomplete. An example of such a situation might be think-ing through policies and investment decisions about the future, in other words strategic thinking.

If you expect to get promoted, eventually you will be required to think strategically. As we saw in Chapter 5, the short term may often be rational but the future is less so. Therefore, as a strategic thinker, you will need both rational and non-rational approaches. You will need help to think about information that currently lacks structure. If you are intu-itive, you will probably grasp the importance of this quite quickly. However, for those of you who are not, let me dwell on this a little more. As a strategic thinker you will be at an advantage if you can approximate which information about the future is most likely to condense into pat-terns and firm frames of reference that you or your organization can either exploit or avoid. As information about the future lacks structure, it is not unreasonable to guess, to use your imagination or to trust your instincts.

Tip If you are not comfortable trusting your gut instincts or your 'feel' for a situation, try to associate with someone who is intuitive.

Answers eventually do condense from future fragments as they move toward the present moment. Your role as a strategic thinker is to see and exploit these to your advantage before someone else.

As an example of unstructured information, consider an open ques-tion. An open-ended question is one that does not or cannot have an answer, yet. Answering the question may be pointless, but examining the contexts that may surround an open-ended question may illuminate blind spots in regard to it. The future is full of open-ended issues that have not yet been resolved. Being able to deal with open-ended questions and to discover any critical blind spots are important strategic thinking skills.

The following idea about how to picture complex relationships involving contexts and incomplete or distant ideas has its origins several hundred years ago. The artist Botticelli depicted a series of inter-related territories in his illustrations of Dante's *Divine*

Answers eventually do condense from future fragments as they move toward the present moment

Comedy drawn more than 500 years ago, circa 1480–95. In these illustrations he created an image of the ascent to heaven, progress being made through higher and higher interrelated circles.

The model below uses the same concepts, that information and people exist with relative circles of influence. *Generally* speaking, we tend not to think about the big picture, because it is so big and because many of the relationships within our big pictures are ill defined and difficult to pin down. The problem with reality is that it can be too big to see. As humans we like to see an edge to situations. We like to know there is a boundary. Sometimes we place the boundary ourselves, close to us for comfort. Where we place those boundaries is a matter for debate, but let me illustrate how we might be compromised by a lack of awareness of where we place limitations within our own thinking.

The onion map

Here is a method for thinking about an open question. Imagine it as a map of interrelated territories, represented by a series of concentric circles. So, for example, if we had to think about reasons why a person might do something, we might begin by labelling from the centre outwards, with (1) representing the person, (2) friends, family and work colleagues, (3) the area, (4) the country, etc. Alternatively, the same sort of map may be used to chart out a business and its connections. An onion has many layers. In this model the number of layers is limitless.

The big onion
(A context map)

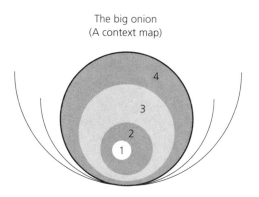

Case study

A particular household lightbulb producer manufactures bulbs for 50 cents and sells them for a dollar. Initially successful in Zone 1 of his context map, our manufacturer expands to sell into Zone 2. In order to fully utilize his factory, he enters Zone 3, which represents the rest of his country.

Our lightbulb maker knows his home market backwards, inside out and upside down. As the current leading supplier, he decides not to supply the whole country because the logistics and investment decisions do not add up. In other words, he has established an edge, a boundary. His current distribution reaches just into Zone 4, but the retailers there have recently been problematic customers, few in number, who seem to be more trouble than they are worth. They complain they cannot sell his product.

Context map and boundaries

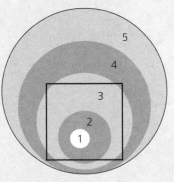

Because our lightbulb maker is focusing hard within his own territory, he has missed a dynamic new competitor in an adjoining country who is moving rapidly from Zone 5 towards Zone 4 and the centre with a product that is much cheaper to produce and also more efficient. By failing to watch the big picture, our original lightbulb maker stands to get wiped out by this new competitor. The original manufacturer's downfall will be his assumption that he knows all he needs to know about the market. The faint voices from the few small dissenting customers at the edge of his business, in Zone 4, were warnings to be heeded.

People set themselves artificial boundaries so that they can simplify and live more easily in their thinking about day-to-day decision making. The problem is that these boundaries are not consciously placed: they are tacitly assumed. This is a useful but potentially dangerous habit in both our social and our business lives. Occasionally literally walking the bounds, making the boundaries explicit and venturing beyond them is advisable.

Using the onion map: Radar thinking

The onion map is very useful for mapping wide-open questions for which only vague information is available. Such a map can help to detect 'where' we are paying most attention and where we may possess blind spots or areas whose possibilities we have not begun to consider.

Most people, when given an open-ended question, will rush at it with several likely answers. Any answer to an open question is, by definition, likely to be a matter of opinion. Rather than address the question, begin thinking about *multiple* contexts and how they relate within the concentric rings of an onion map.

Any answer to an open question is, by definition, likely to be a matter of opinion

When using this tool, the priority is to map multiple *possibilities*, not answers. Rushing in without considering the nature of the question delivers some results but in a haphazard and less efficient way. It is far more productive to first lay out a map of the various related zones surrounding the issue and then consider several possibilities within each zone. The answers will fall into categories. There will be more answers about which we feel sure or more familiar. Usually gaps become apparent. By looking at the whole range of interrelated possibilities, we can use a 'radar' approach to thinking to illuminate first where our boundaries might have been set and secondly any gaps or blind spots in our thinking.

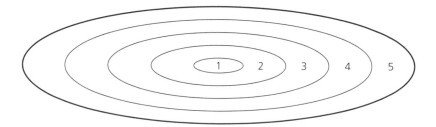

For example, if a group of people are given the problem of suggesting reasons for the mysterious disappearance of a middle-aged man, the zones would build outwards from (1) the person, (2) his immediate family and friends, (3) work, (4) area, (5) district, (6) region, (7) country, and (8) continent. (People usually stop there but it is possible to continue: (9) planet, (10) galaxy, and (11) universe!) It is then easier to drop suggested reasons into all zones of possibility.

> **Tip** You will know when you have produced enough outer rings when the contexts become funny, as in the example above. You should ensure this point is reached, otherwise the boundaries may fall short of reality. Also make sure the centre is reduced to the simplest element. On occasion the mapping process can get messy. Don't worry about this – you can always tidy it up later. Sometimes there may be several maps overlapped.

Of itself this tool does not provide answers, but it does help us map where we are paying attention, our boundaries and where we have blind spots. This tool is particularly useful when dealing with strategic planning where there are many unknown issues to consider.

In summary

When we are faced with complicated situations, we need the ability to think through and deal with unstructured information. Learning to live with un-answered questions and adopting a mature attitude to control and collabora-tion are as important as having the ability to model unstructured information in our mind. When we think about a complex context we might visualize egg shapes or onions or frames, but we must always remember that other people will have different world views, sometimes with quite different boundaries. Being able to see over the horizon is the job of your radar system. An onion model or, if you prefer, Botticelli's illustration of celestial rings each linked to a higher order, can provide you with a template for thinking about unstructured information.

Political awareness and scanning for soft as well as hard information are important attributes if you wish to be in charge of something significant. Two very important behaviours that help us deal with complexity are net-working and mentoring.

If we aspire to rise up through an organization or to increase our influence, we must learn to deal with incomplete information and to think strategically. Any strategic thinking process requires the ability to look forwards in time and to predict future risks and opportunity. Again, this will involve dealing with fragmented information. Strategic thinking ability requires imagination to create something useful out of such fragments. With this in mind, the next chapter provides some tools to aid with thinking creatively.

How to get the big idea: Creativity

11

U sing imagery as an aid, this book began with a variety of tools to help us think about increasingly non-rational and ultimately diffuse concepts such as ambiguity, uncertainty and the future. By putting divergent ideas into a series of models I started to build a bridgehead between the rational and the illogical.

Rational thinking tools are useful in day-to-day management situations. However, in order to have a well-rounded thinking repertoire we must be able to exercise our creativity. If we are able to apply this, we can improve the quality of options we create in ambiguous circumstances and really start to take control of our future. Also, with the aid of a little imagination we can begin to make sense out of vague information, we can create strategies to confound our competitors and, of course, creativity can be of great service in negotiation and problem solving.

Creativity takes an open, divergent thinking pathway. (See Chapter 2 on focused and divergent thinking.) The purpose of this chapter is to introduce you to how to develop divergent ways of thinking. These introductory techniques are designed to encourage original thought and to develop choices. If we remain rational, we can become predictable in our activities. Original strategy and solutions are derived from original thought, which requires creativity and imagination.

When we are aware of more than one choice, we build resilience and strength into a business or our personal lives. In learning to take a broader perspective we can develop a wider perception of current and future business possibilities and risks. Creative thinking, properly applied, can pay enormous dividends.

Focused versus wide-open thinking

We saw in Chapter 2 how many businesses are involved in delivering 'here and now' results to their customers and how results-driven organizations need to employ people who are task focused in order to deliver their promises. Someone who is predisposed to a convergent or focused thinking pattern is more likely to be attractive as an employee than a divergent, creative thinker simply because they are capable of focusing their minds and their behaviours on delivering 'here and now'; they are results orientated and work wonderfully when the work they are doing 'fits' the current set of rules or paradigm.

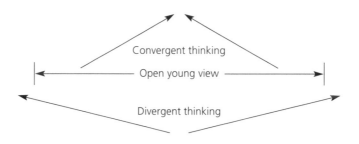

By contrast, working with creative people who prefer a divergent thinking pathway is not easy. The obvious benefit of using good, divergent, wide-open thinkers is that they are often excellent at generating a variety of ideas and alternatives. However, divergent thinkers, by their nature, may find other creative thinkers difficult to track, so team working is likely to be a problem. The temptation to work on newer or more exciting novel ideas may overwhelm their ability to complete something. People with naturally creative minds may find it difficult to work within conventional constraints or in a disciplined system.

Much of present-day society places pressures on people to focus and conform within disciplined systems. Our results-based, consumer-driven, exam-passing society enhances the likelihood of people adopting focused thinking patterns.

The very best thinkers are those who are either born with the ability to, or learn to, master both focused or convergent thinking *and* creative divergent patterns. People who are natural convergent and divergent thinkers are often intuitive entrepreneurs and innovators. The good news is that it is possible to learn how to think creatively at any age in life.

Develop an open frame of mind

Most young children are quite comfortable with the fact that they have huge gaps in their knowledge and that the world is an ambiguous place. As we grow older, we seek to reduce the uncomfortable ambiguity in life by reducing the unknown and seeking out certainties: we go for control at the expense of openness.

One of the early lessons in thinking creatively is to suspend the rulebook completely

Assumptions, rules and routines are established and gradually we achieve a level of comfort through a sense of certainty. The cost of this certainty may be a limitation on our imagination. So one of the early lessons in thinking creatively is to suspend the rulebook completely.

Tip Try this for a while, especially during a creativity session. When you feel compelled to question, contradict or oppose a view from someone else, place your tongue between your teeth and hold it there. Recognize any inner frustration and simply let go of it. You can do this by accepting that the other person has a right to hold the view that they do, but – at the same time – you also have your equal right to your own different view. Once you have reached this level of acceptance, try to accept that more than one alternative can co-exist for the same subject. Once you are here, then try to entertain the notion that you may need to change your own view partially or completely.

Emotion and creativity

When we cross the edge of a frame of reference there are two major types of emotional reaction. The vast majority of people will laugh, but in a very small number of cases some people will get angry.

Laugh!

Young children have bright, hungry minds that are very capable of dealing with divergent thought processes. Divergent thinking is playful thinking. However, as we mature, we employ increasingly focused thinking skills. Notice that children laugh a lot more than adults do. Also notice that when we laugh we 'are at the edge' of socially acceptable ideas or we may be completely out of our comfort zones. Jokes are no longer funny when we 'know' them. In children's lives there is a lot of ambiguity because many of their information needs have not yet been met. There is a lot of uncertainty but more room for magic! Magic is made possible in the imagination. There is joy in discovery and learning. As we adopt rational learning methods based on certainties, the magic disappears, for two reasons. The first is we are no longer 'at the edge', and secondly we are employing much more critical focused thinking.

People laugh to relieve tension and to express enjoyment. Laughter also signals to other people a positive attitude to the ambiguity in a situation. When we laugh, we express our tacit permission to cross over or alter the boundaries for a while. Laughter can indicate pain too. Some people will laugh when they are distressed. They too are at 'the edge' or beyond the natural boundaries of their frames of reference.

If the creative thinking process fails to provoke strong feelings then it will probably not be productive

We saw in Chapter 3 that our frames of reference are really useful, but that they can be traps that blindside our thinking to new opportunities and potential risks. In order to escape a fixed frame of reference we must be prepared to cross over the limiting boundaries. This usually means we will need to laugh and play. If the creative thinking process fails to provoke strong feelings such as laughter or a sense of tension then it will probably not be productive.

> **Tip** When you laugh, be aware of what caused the humour and try to stay with it.

Anger

Anger seems to be aroused in two different sorts of situation, fortunately both rare. The first potential hotspot in creative thinking workshops is when someone feels their personal value system has been stepped on, causing them deep offence. The second type of situation seems to be about a personal sense of control. A few people, typically strong controllers, may feel increasingly uncomfortable with an apparent lack of structure or direction. This anger is not a reaction to what is being said, but to the alarm they feel in their perception that their boundaries are being removed. Creativity has a lot to do with moving beyond the rational frames of reference that shape our thinking. Non-rational thinking can be great fun for the majority, but for a very few people moving away from their day-to-day control or comfort zone can feel very unsafe.

These difficulties can be reduced by highlighting in the introduction to any creativity session what people may feel, by commenting that occasionally strong feelings may be experienced as a normal reaction and by showing a route map. My advice for people who want control is to try to see the benefit others derive from its temporary removal and learn to allow the flow towards new concepts to take place. Any attempt to return to 'disciplined structure' will cut off the flow of good ideas. The best thing for people to do here if they feel angry or unsafe is to take a walk. So before you begin a creativity session, give people clear, unambiguous permission to leave and return at any time – no request or explanation required.

Holding creativity sessions: Good practice

To help people who need structure in their thinking, always provide a process map and basic rules. My first rule, as just mentioned, is that the activity is entirely optional and anyone is free to leave and rejoin at any time without explanation. The second rule is that there are many crossing points over the borders of a frame of reference and any player has the right to ask the group to cross somewhere else. *Generally* speaking, when engaging creativity exercises it is best to avoid rules.

Here are a few more useful pointers.

Ownership

Assuming you have clearly identified the issue, there has to be someone who is willing to give a commitment to solving the problem; otherwise the exercise is only ever seen as just play. Ideally there should be ownership by someone specific with a clear, well-defined ability to act after ideas are discovered. This person should be identified before the session starts.

How to make creativity work for you

- Push beyond the obvious; resist the temptation to ease off the tension by providing easy, obvious answers. Stay with the awkwardness – it's OK.

- If you hear yourself offering up standard management-textbook answers, you are comfortably back inside the frame of reference and you will have lost the power of the process. To counteract this, stay in touch with the obscure, the ridiculous and the bizarre.

- Do not question or analyze. Avoid being negative; restate problems or negatives as 'how to ...'.
- Be honest and speak only for yourself; do not paraphrase or take over what other people say.
- Try to listen to your intuition – offer up ideas and do not try to explain them.
- Listen and try to interpret the best in what is said – keep an open mind.
- No competing.
- Do not try to lead.
- Do not try to take control.
- Try not to organize the information being produced; in fact a little chaos can promote more fun and serendipitous discovery.

Patience

In addition, individual and group players must learn to be patient and wait till the end of a creativity session for a *suggestion* of interesting answers, not *complete* answers. Creativity mostly sets our minds on the track of interesting clues. Ideas will often be born with flaws and any amount of premature analysis will cause the idea to shrivel on the spot. Ideas need to be incubated long enough for you to spot their potential to be combined or used as new insights to reinforce another good idea or repair a flaw.

> **Tip** Creativity sessions can be a little false. Our minds sometimes like to incubate an idea, so be prepared for ideas to arrive in your mind after the formal end of the session.

Unhelpful phrases

The following phrases should be considered unacceptable during idea-generating sessions:

- 'Can I ask ...?'
- 'We've thought of that already.'

- 'We've tried that already.'
- 'That's been done before.'
- 'It can't be done.'
- 'It won't work because ...'
- 'It's not allowed.'
- 'It's the same as ...'

The old maxim of thinking of three good reasons to support an idea before you earn the right to criticize it may be useful outside of a creativity session, but no 'rights' of criticism of any sort should be allowed during idea formulation. Asking questions of others is therefore not acceptable. Difficulties can be examined by rephrasing them as 'how to ...' statements.

Go for volume

To avoid analysis, select what you consider to be the simplest statement about the creative need and then generate as many ideas as possible, later following through with a vigorous selection process. In most creativity sessions, well over 95 per cent of the output will be of no use and will be dumped. So to be productive, you need to create as much volume as possible to generate a few gems. It only takes a small number of excellent ideas to solve a problem or to form a novel strategy to deliver sustainable commercial advantage.

In most creativity sessions, well over 95 per cent of the output will be of no use

Being 'an expert' can be a disadvantage when it comes to developing new ideas. Encourage diversity in the selection of a creativity project team; outsiders can be very helpful.

Collecting in ideas and concepts: Harvesting

This is the most important part of the process and the point at which you can begin the journey towards familiar, conventional thinking territory. You now begin to collect, refine and reduce the ideas and concepts so that you now are aware of a wide range of choices or of subtle systems that can be exploited.

Sometimes people, having enjoyed a playful outward journey, rush back to conventional thinking and the power of creativity quickly dissipates as creative tension is suddenly reduced. Creative answers are not deduced by comfortable logic but from awkward, irrational tensions. Slowing the return journey is a very important aspect of using the creative tension to pull out sensible meaning from abstract thoughts.

At this stage of thinking, many possible solutions are usually not in a completed or refined form. Early ideas, while they may show good direction and unique possibilities, will also be wide open to criticism because they are only half born and possibly ill formed. Handle with care and protect them at this stage. A separate note of the bizarre may prove useful later – if only as a trigger for another creativity session.

By the end, the output will be cut down to just a few major themes and ideas, which will then serve as drivers for new strategies, products or processes. The process described above should have helped to define two or three new opportunities that were previously partly hidden. Once a new direction or opportunity is identified, conventional, rational decision processes can be re-engaged.

Creative thinking tools – the basic process

There are many ways to be creative. All of the methods I use involve the creation of high levels of ambiguity and then forcing our minds to make creative sense of what we find. There is usually a five-step process, which takes people on a trip powered by the imagination far, far away from the issue and then, staying mentally open, we move slowly but creatively back in the general direction of common-sense territory. This distinction between directions is important because a high degree of openness is required in both. The outward journey is always great fun but the homeward-bound, idea-discovery phase involves a sense of tension. This last step is where people have to fight to hold off their critical and analytical processes and at the same time discover new ideas. The easy but wrong approach at this last stage is to go for obvious connections with rational possibilities.

Five-stage creativity process map

- State the problem as simply as possible. No analysis allowed. Then forget it for a while. Point out to the group that you will return to it later.

- Play, ensure fun and, in particular, promote laughter. The process does *not* work well if there is no laughter, fun or sense of elation. Creativity *is* an emotional exercise. It is also quite exhausting because boundaries are down.

- Having collected some bizarre ideas that are truly 'remote' from the original issue, ask people to force out solutions that are in some odd way connected with the remote ideas they have just produced. Usually this comes as a fun shock, since people's minds are presented with a highly novel situation. When faced with highly entertaining novelty, our minds work very hard to resolve such contradictions. It is important to slow the journey 'home' to prevent too early a re-entry to the frame of reference. Quite often the essence of a good idea can be quickly turned into banalities by rational thought processes which quickly crop the novelty out of an idea. So try to *stay out* of the frame for as long as possible; stick with novelty and do not accept the obvious answers.

- Harness the best ideas, stay loose, do not get at all judgemental yet and see if any of the ideas can be combined or improved. Most original ideas will have flaws of some sort.

- Try to understand the power within each idea by understanding its underpinning concept (see 'Working with concepts and ideas' below).

Creative thinking methods

There are many creative thinking tools available. Here are three methods I find work well in my hands:

- random words
- assumption busting
- rich pictures.

The notes that follow are aimed at getting you to try to exercise your own creative thinking skills. You cannot learn how to ride a bicycle or to play soccer by reading a book alone; you have to mount the bicycle or pick up the ball and have a go. Then practise, practise, practise. Practice improves performance. If you want to learn how to be creative, the same rule applies.

These methods can be used either by individuals or groups. Often two heads are better than one, so try if you can to think through an opportunity or a problem with the participation of a friend or colleague.

Most of these exercises take between 45 and 75 minutes.

You have to mount the bicycle or pick up the ball and have a go

Method 1: Random word exercise

Define your problem or opportunity simply, then forget it for 20 minutes or so.

Pick at random (do not select) three words from a dictionary or any other rich word source. Ideally this should not be a book from your regular experience.

Write down each of these words on a clean piece of paper. Then, for each word, spread your thinking by putting on paper whatever thoughts or images the word produces in your mind.

Continue by extending the best of the words by free word association and adding new words or images, either as a group or alone. Spend approximately 20 minutes having fun with the process. Do *not* look for any answers to the problem at this stage. Use, enjoy and play with anything that stimulates a sense of fun. Try not to dwell on which words or images you create – move quickly and freely. Indulge yourself for 15 or 20 minutes and feel free to laugh and to enjoy what you are doing!

If working in a group of five or six people, each person picks a powerful suggestive word or image from the output of the whole group. Pick one that makes you feel something! If you are working alone, draw out any five words that appeal to you. Allocate your choice(s) to a big clean space.

Then select one powerful word or image to work on. Start to 'force' this onto the issue you need an answer to. This step may involve a little further extension but now remember that the goal is to force out several connections, however abstract. 'Play' with a chosen word or image until you get bored or have exhausted its potential, then pick another of your chosen words or images to connect to your original problem.

The next step is the really demanding part. Do not be tempted to rush back into conventional solutions. You may feel awkward, even frustrated, but try to maintain this feeling of 'tension' as a useful tool to stimulate your mind. If you do feel uncomfortable, don't worry – tension is normal when you are learning without boundaries.

The raised attention levels stimulated by the ambiguity and tension will demand a lot of energy, so expect to feel tired after any creativity exercise.

You are more likely to develop partial answers or clues – phrases such as 'We believe the answer may have something to do with …' or 'may possibly involve …'. As you progress, ideas can be quickly tested for novelty value. Weak ideas will be easily copied or predicted by a competitor. If your answers are sounding too conventional, try to make more of the ambiguity promoted by the bizarre words. Be brave!

Method 2: Assumption buster

Our frames of reference are built up of what we regard as facts or truths. These facts are often assumptions that will remain true for a while; however, over time several will change or become less fixed without our noticing. We continue to think of these as valid, *fixed* truths when in fact they are not. Playfulness can liberate us from our preconceptions. A game of assumption busting can be used as a way of escaping our assumptions.

The aim of this game is to test our deepest assumptions. One way to do this is to create huge 'lies' about the assumptions we generally believe to be true. We bring the lie into reality and imagine that our bizarre suggestions are actually true. Then we play with the lie and consider how we could enrich the evolution of the new situation. By playing with a lie we learn to re-position previously hidden assumptions that may have blocked us in some way. If the lies are huge or bizarre enough, the game becomes even more creative and can lead to original insights. After 20 minutes of play with a chosen lie, we look for interesting lessons that may prove useful in the real world. Sometimes these lessons are component parts that work immediately in the real world; sometimes the lessons come through the medium of an analogy.

This is how it works. Define the problem or the opportunity simply, then forget about it for 20 minutes or so.

Develop a list of as many assumptions as you can think of. Select a few you suspect could be interesting and then 'bust' them. Assumptions become 'lies' when we change them significantly, for example by flipping them over to mean something else, by reversing roles, by exaggeration or by subtraction of part or all of the assumption. Meaning can be distorted by making the assumption true for only a very limited or a very long time. Alternatively true meaning can be distorted by making the assumption true but only for a different quantity.

Pick the three most bizarre conversions or the ones you like best and treat each one separately. Start a conversation in which you imagine the effects of making the lie reality. The conversation usually gathers pace, so try to write some notes on the development as it goes along. See where the lie leads. Usually the more bizarre ideas can go through several steps until they become very funny or surreal. The group should treat each suggestion as absolutely real and should attempt to imagine what it would mean in practical terms to really implement each bizarre idea. Extend the consequences as widely as possible and see what happens.

The simpler, obvious distortions tend not to lead anywhere useful. Therefore push the boundaries and use the outrageous or bizarre ideas first. To get into this technique, it has to be fun! It is important that all the team imagines a world in which all of the rules can be re-written. Get into the character and feeling of the new situation and sense what you would see, hear and feel in the new worlds you create. If any of the ideas become outrageously macabre, try a 180-degree flip. This means you restate the macabre idea as its extreme positive opposite and continue from there.

Push the boundaries and use the outrageous or bizarre ideas first

Do not worry if the ideas are incomplete: you can build them up later. When you are having enough fun with the distortions of current assumptions you should be a great distance from reality. Now force your mind to come to useful conclusions about what can be done in the real world using the best parts of the ideas within the bizarre realities you generated. This process has the benefit of making us think more carefully about the useful attributes of the component parts of an idea or situation.

Finally consider what could be added, reinforced or combined to produce several improved ideas.

It is *very* important that at the end of the session you destroy any notes that no longer serve a purpose simply because no one from outside the process would be able to make a reasonable interpretation of them.

Assumption busting tends to be a less bizarre process than the random word approach, and I find that people who prefer high structure in their thinking enjoy this more than the random word method. Assumption busting is quite good for thinking about policy as well as products.

Method 3: Rich pictures

This is quite simple and again involves playing with tacit assumptions from our subconscious. This is applied 'doodling', but on a massive scale! You need ideally as big a piece of paper as possible, plus lots of colouring materials, objects, magazines and accessories.

Drawing in any colour (no words allowed) and using any image whatsoever, first produce, on the left-hand third of your paper, images relating to the present. Then, on the right-hand third, draw and colour representations of the future. Then in between the two sections draw the transition imagery. Then draw in route maps from present to future.

The drawing phase may take about 30 minutes or so. When it is complete, ask for interpretation, meanings, lessons and opportunities.

Rich pictures can produce quite liberating ideas *if* other people are actually ready for them. In my experience some people will tend to be introspective toward the organization whereas others with a more strategic view will depict or expect external issues. If you plan to use rich pictures, provide your team with a little guidance at the beginning as to the scope of the exercise and where to place most of their attention. Care should be taken, however, not to constrain people too much.

There are multiple other creative thinking tools that help our thinking along a divergent pathway. Where possible, encourage people with diverse backgrounds to be members of creativity workshops. Also where possible, encourage the use of an outside facilitator skilled in running high-value creativity workshops.

Working with concepts and ideas

There is one other important frontier that needs to be addressed when considering creative thinking. People talk about concepts and ideas, but do not always properly understand the difference between them. While they are related, they are significantly different in terms of their power.

There is a huge difference between the power of an idea and the power of a concept. A concept is always significantly more influential and much more valuable. If you can learn to discover the concept that underpins an idea, you will be better informed and more likely to deliver a wider, more interesting range of choices.

For example, in my thinking skills workshops I run an exercise which involves unpacking a whole series of concepts that underpin certain business ideas. The ideas I use to start from are the price points and offers from different types of business. I then ask people to clearly identify three aspects of a particular business. In their answers we can see a pattern emerge as to what people are actually paying for. When people pay for a product or service, they often actually pay for a bundle of experiences. This bundle of experiences we may sum up in a few words. If you can find a few words that capture the richer meaning, this is a concept.

Learning to think in terms of concepts instead of ideas takes the intellectual process to a much higher

> **If you can learn to discover the concept that underpins an idea, you will be better informed and more likely to deliver a wider, more interesting range of choices**

level. This ability can be highly beneficial to anyone who wants to be creative. For example, innovation is not always simply about the application of a brand-new technology. Very often, innovation can be a unique reconfiguration of currently available methods and technologies. Therefore mapping and developing a closer understanding of currently available concepts can be a quick way of finding powerful new starting points.

Concept workout

Try this thinking exercise for yourself: it's easy. We are going to invent a new eating-out experience. Draw three columns on a page. The first is headed 'What', i.e. the idea; the second (broad) column is headed 'Concept', i.e. why people choose this food outlet; and the third (narrow) column is headed 'Price', meaning the inclusive price for two people. If we decide to develop a new chain of restaurants we can easily identify what the current ideas are, for example pizza, Thai, Chinese, curry, Italian, Japanese, and so on. Likewise approximate prices are easy to estimate. Unpacking the concepts, though, tends to be more elusive, but ultimately very worthwhile. If a meal for two were approximately the same price, why would someone choose one type above another? What different experience would they expect to find?

When we examine ideas we will find something tangible: something quite specific can be identified or seen, such as a pizza or being served by an Italian waiter. The specificity of the idea lends clarity but significantly narrows the potential for further development. When we deal with a concept, however, such as 'impressing other people' or 'luxury' or 'invoking holiday atmosphere', we find we are dealing with a force that comes fully loaded with multiple possibilities. You get more 'bangs for your bucks' with a concept than you do with an idea. With this in mind when you are being creative, go hunting for rich ideas, then try to think about the concepts whence they spring. This is the rich seam to mine to multiply one idea into many others.

The exercise can be completed by looking at the component parts of the currently available concepts, reconfiguring them, taking away something or introducing new elements and setting new price points to invent new eating experiences.

In summary

There are a variety of ways to think creatively. All of them involve a thinking journey that denies current reality in some way. When we force our minds to make an unreasonable connection between bizarre ideas and the issue we are working on, we create a level of novelty that our minds will work hard to resolve. Feelings are *always* involved in creative thinking exercises. If there is no sense of fun, the level of creativity is likely to be low. Giving permission to enjoy yourself is essential.

Creativity should not be a one-off exercise reserved for 'crazy away days'. This style of thinking should be regularly employed to ensure that what you do is currently valid, wise and imaginative. Thinking is hard work, especially creative thinking. Expect to feel tired if you use your mind at the edge. If we don't exercise this particular mental muscle, our minds and our lives will grow flabby.

There are many ways and means to think, but without imagination life is an austere, bone-dry, dull place. Of all the attributes a manager must possess beyond everyday implementation skills, I would say a sense of humour, humility and the ability to think and act with imagination to inspire other people are all at or close to the top of the list. In my opinion any organization that fails to have these skills represented at all levels will be punished in fast-moving, high-value markets. If people are to be inspired to follow a great strategy, you will need the powers of imagination and self-expression.

Know yourself, then conquer 　　12

This book is about moving from monochrome to colour, from monotone to quadraphonic, from flat, two-dimensional thinking to the vibrance of three dimensions. It is essential to build our thinking skills because we are living in an increasingly competitive world, in which message intensity grows relentlessly and where more people seem to expect our attention and our best efforts on their behalf. Even when we return to our personal lives, the standards of what is expected of us are pushed higher by increasingly pervasive media and social norm forming. So how do we thrive? We learn to think and work smarter.

The maths behind the number of hours *actually* worked by many managers are appalling. Some people put in 40 years' work for 30 years' pay. Put another way, they lose ten of their best years. Of course some retire early. However, others burn out or worse, from an overindulgence towards the needs of others. I'm not suggesting that working long hours is necessarily a bad thing, so long as you have given serious thought to the tradeoff. Some people love their work while others feel increasingly driven by it. Clearly if you are honestly passionate about what you are doing, are sure that the social life you have supports you fully and, at the same time, are able to attend fully to the needs of important people in your personal life, then go ahead: put the time in – but smartly.

How do we do this? There are many aspects to our lives for which we are not well prepared by our formal education. One of these is the way we think. Rational, structured logic we can acquire because it is a normal, everyday transaction in colleges and at work. There is, however, little guidance on how to think through complex subjects that seem to defy logic. In the preceding chapters of *How to Think* I have gone some of the way to specifically addressing a variety of neglected areas for which the rational thought process seems not to work too well. No matter what we choose to do with our lives, we will face:

- complexities
- politics
- issues to do with truth and deceit
- ambiguity and uncertainty
- alternative perceptions
- unstructured information
- contradictions
- a need to be creative
- a need to inspire others in difficult times
- our own mistakes

and we must learn how to cope with increasing complexity.

Throughout the book I have used the overarching concept that images as well as words can help us to think in a smarter way. Using shapes realigns us with our instincts. Because our instincts involve rapid-reaction systems and often higher energy states, learning how to access them as part of our everyday thinking can improve our performance. Many of the education and employment systems within our society have led us towards an over-dependence upon rational, structured logic. If we are to thrive in a complex future, we will need to demonstrate intellectual agility and the ability to use non-rational, illogical thinking methods as well.

Learning how to think involves allowing our minds sufficient time and space to stretch and to remain sufficiently open before we come to conclusions. We realize that the world is dynamic and alive and that our ideas and attitudes need to remain fresh and alert. Time has an influence too. A right decision five years ago is not necessarily still a right decision today.

Decision-making ability is important to us all. If we get largely right some of the bigger decisions in our life then our time may be harmonious. Of course we will all make some mistakes along the way. The important lesson here is to realize that mistakes should be learning opportunities, not the subjects of guilt and shame. True, luck occasionally plays its part, but I believe we should not surrender to it. Continuous learning and adjusting our perception to accommodate new lessons is part of everyone's life. Learning to think is a lifelong task. It doesn't stop.

Our minds are fabulous places. They can become richly furnished, exciting palaces or they can be left with doors unguarded for other people's ideas to come squatting. Learning to think means taking responsibility for our present perception, for our own thoughts, for the mind food we take in and for our choices and actions.

In order to be an effective player in any game we need to be fit. Thinking is no exception. To be fit, we need to exercise, test, check and work out. Often exercise with others helps us to step up the pace.

> **Our minds can become richly furnished, exciting palaces or they can be left with doors unguarded for other people's ideas to come squatting**

Tip If you are able to do so, discuss the models or the tips in this book with someone you trust. In this way your mind has time to embed the ideas into your thinking. Better still, learning is enhanced even further if you try to teach someone what you have discovered.

The Confucian wisdom of 'Know yourself first and then conquer' points us toward a fundamental aspect of thinking, namely the need to know where we are coming from and what is shaping our direction. This knowledge is something we should review throughout our lives. Our perceptions can, given enough time, be improved or enhanced. Wholesale changes in the nature of the way we think, and of who we are, are unlikely and become even less so as we age. We can, however, make the most of the thinking capacity we are endowed with – at any age.

There is another basic aspect of thinking skills that you need to be aware of. When building mental muscle, we begin with self-awareness and learn the art of separation. What we separate in our transactions with ourselves and others is a choice we can make. While emotion should not rule our lives, it does have a role in enriching them and should not be denied. Take away all emotion and you may well be successful in business but you will also be a pale imitation of life. Also, deny who you really are in favour of a false goal and you will end up frustrated and empty. I'm not suggesting you drop out and follow your life's dream to, for example, sell everything and become a potter sitting in California. What I am saying is that your chances of higher levels of performance, and perhaps happiness, rest upon coming to know your deeper goals, and being true to them.

A poor life this if, full of care,
We have no time to stand and stare.
WILLIAM HENRY DAVIES, 1871–1940, 'LEISURE'

Finally, life's bigger rewards are not all material. When you reflect upon the higher-value aspects of life, you will see they are mostly there for free. When you begin to see this every day, it will be symptomatic of your working smarter, not harder.

Supplementary notes and recommended reading

Chapter 1

If you have decided life is already too intense, reading may not be the best first step! So go do some yoga or t'ai chi, chop logs, walk the dog or go for a swim. Once you've created some space for yourself to read, see *If Life is a Game These Are the Rules* by Cherie Carter Scott, published 1999 by Hodder & Stoughton. Also try Dr Richard Carlson's bestseller *Don't Sweat the Small Stuff ... and It's All Small Stuff,* published 1997 by Hyperion and 1998 by Hodder & Stoughton.

If you like the idea of visualization and self-renewal, try Jack Black's self-help book *Mindstore*, published 1994 by Thorsons/HarperCollins.

Chapter 2

For the terms **convergent and divergent thinking**, see J.P. Guildford's *The Nature of Intelligence*, published 1967 by McGraw-Hill, New York. These terms are subsequently used in Liam Hudson's *Contrary Imaginations*, published 1967 by Penguin.

On **shopping**. Retailers really do go out of their way to understand customer patterns of behaviour. For example, see 'Winning Customer Ownership – the Jaeger Service Excellence Story' by Doug Griffin, published in *Managing Service Quality* 1997, pp. 80–6. This paper demonstrates the lengths a company will go to to know and serve its customers. Few spend less than 30 minutes in a Jaeger shop; many spend one to two hours.

On **multitasking**, I tried, in vain, to follow up a story mentioned during a BBC programme about speed that suggested that women scored better than men in aptitude tests for managing multiple systems in complex aircraft. This seems logical. Women are usually better at multitasking than men, but does this mean they would make better fighter pilots? There are significant differences between men and women and, when harnessed, such differences can be complementary. If we understand the different styles and resources available to other people, the chances for complementary team working are enhanced.

Our education system, together with the orientation of Western industry, has led much of the workforce to a predominantly 'focus' approach to thinking. As we adopt faster technology, the requirement for multitasking is likely to increase. Returning to the notion of combat aircraft, according to another TV programme, the latest Euro-fighter aircraft has addressed the average male need for simplicity. According to the programme, most of this aircraft's systems have been reduced so that all the pilot has to do is fly and talk with a female-voiced computer. The plane is so fast that the computer makes over 200 adjustments per second to the wings. The multitasking element has been managed out of that particular system.

Chapter 3

On **frames of reference**, see 'Strategy and Creative Thinking in Business' by Stephen Reid, Chapter 17 of *Exploring Techniques of Analysis and Evaluation in Strategic Management*, edited by Veronique Ambrosini with Gerry Johnson and Kevin Scholes, published 1998 by Prentice Hall.

On **parallel error**, see Gareth Bryan-Jones, *Orienteering Techniques*, Scottish Orienteering Association, 1994.

Chapter 4

There are several sources of interesting material to read on the subject of the **innermost workings of our minds**. Your personal values provide a sense of meaning and are an important source of motivation. The knowledge and understanding of your inner values, goals and motivations feature in a wide range of books by a variety of different types of author. Here are some books that I recommend.

Like a million other readers, I have been impressed and inspired by Stephen R. Coveys' bestseller *The Seven Habits of Highly Effective People*, first published in the UK in 1992 by Simon & Schuster.

Also there is a whole swathe of books clustered around beliefs to do with 'NLP' or **'Neuro-Linguistic Programming'**. There are some aspects of NLP that make me uncomfortable and I also disagree with several of the basic ideas within the NLP school. Despite these reservations, I find that the NLP camp is also home to some very good common-sense ideas. I can recommend sections within any of the following that deal with values and with the deeper processes that motivate you: Joseph O'Connor and John Seymour, *Introducing NLP, Neuro-Linguistic Programming*, published by Mandala and Thorsons in 1995; Shelle Rose Charvet, *Words that Change Minds*, published 1995, 1997 by Kendall/Hunt, Iowa.

Also, there are a variety of **self-development** exercises in Steve Andreas's and Charles Faulkner's book *The NLP Comprehensive Training Team – NLP, The New Technology of Achievement*, published 1994 by Quill, William Morrow, New York.

Liz Simpson's book *Working from the Heart*, published 1999 by Vermillion, is a 'can do' sort of self-development book. Liz points out how a 'poverty consciousness' can limit self-development and goes on to develop the possibility that we can 're-script' our lives.

Chapter 5

The analogy of mountaineers, trauma zones and the **dangerous edge** comes from two British psychologists. Steve Carter at Apter International developed the analogy based upon his colleague Michael J. Apter's book *The Dangerous Edge – The Psychology of Excitement*, published 1992 by The Free Press, New York.

On **scenario planning**, a really easy-to-read and informative book as a starting point is *The Art of the Long View* by Peter Schwartz, published 1996 by Wiley. For practitioners, the most comprehensive yet easy-to-read overview of scenario planning I have read is Gill Ringland's *Scenario Planning – Managing for the Future*, published 1998, also by Wiley.

Chapter 6

Problem types and problem solving. In Charles Handy's excellent book *The Empty Raincoat*, published 1994 by Arrow Business Books, Charles makes mention of Type 1 and Type 2 errors. The first is a failure pure and simple, while the second is a failure to fully exploit or develop what is available. In other words, the opportunity is not maximized. This suggests that there are at least two types of problem or opportunity to begin with, one with a defined specific outcome, the other open ended. Both types of problems have right answers, but in the second case some responses are more right than others. Problem types are also considered in Peter M. Senge's *The 5th Discipline*, published 1990 by Currency Doubleday, New York. Peter mentions two classes of problem, detail and dynamic. The first can be precisely resolved by study, but the second cannot because the nature of the problem itself is open to multiple interpretations. On the basis of these two works I synthesized the idea of a maximal and a slippery problem. The work by Barry Johnson on Polarities (see reference under Chapter 7) identifies a further class of dilemma in which diametrically opposed choices cannot be separated without significant loss. In a sense these problems are joined at the hip. This third class of problem cannot be separately resolved and they need to be managed together within a contradiction.

For a wide-ranging review of methods of problem solving, see Arthur B. Grundy Jr, *Techniques of Structured Problem Solving*, published 1980 and 1988 by Van Nostrand Reinhold, New York. If you would like to look at creative approaches to problem solving, see the recommendations under Chapter 11. For those of you who enjoy complex problem solving, look at books to do with **systems thinking**. For example, Senge's *The 5th Discipline* (cited above) is excellent. A book by Joseph O'Connor and Ian McDermott, *The Art of Systems Thinking*, published 1997 by Thorsons, has some useful ideas. If you are really and truly keen then there is a society of 'systematologists' who publish a members' journal.

In my limited experience, the general difficulty with systems thinking is that the models look seductively easy to understand after someone else has worked them out. Deducing elegantly simple models out of complex situations, however, is not at all easy. Systems maps can be very worthwhile and can produce remarkable insights.

Chapter 7

All organizations face the need to make fundamental decisions. If people are highly risk averse, decision making may be inhibited and managers limited in their ability to evolve good decisions. In Chapter 7 we looked at two models of different cultural orientations towards error that could help us appreciate alternative perspectives. **Cultural differences** are neither arbitrary nor uniform. There are many different characteristics that may be attributed to a culture. The act of describing 'culture' is laden with difficulty, for example subjective opinion, racial stereotyping, historical misrepresentation and other problems cloud the picture. There are a variety of cultural measures available and, because I am by no means an expert in this area, I am unable to make useful comparisons. However, I recently met with Charles Hampton Turner, and his work together with Fons Trompenaars on cultural difference looks impressive and compares many different countries.

The research by Charles Hampton Turner and Fons Trompenaars forms a significant body of work on how managers from different countries deal with dilemmas. Their research shows there are verifiable patterns that can inform us of how different nationalities *generally* tend to think. I would particularly recommend *21 Leaders for the 21st Century*, published 2001 by Capstone, and *Building Cross-Cultural Competence*, published 2000 by Wiley.

There are lots of references available on **3M**. One of the most easily accessible insights into their prevailing operating philosophy in the mid-1990s comes from an easy-to-read pamphlet called *The UK Innovation Lecture 5/3/96 – Building a Tradition of Innovation*, DTI (Department of Trade and Industry in the UK) booklet URN 96/619. Dr William Coyne, a senior executive from 3M, was the guest speaker for the UK 1996 DTI-sponsored Innovation Lecture, delivered to several thousand British managers through satellite links.

Chapter 8

Ralph Bedrock worked with me in the late 1990s to develop a **rich-picture** exercise with 100 local government senior managers. Ralph introduced me to the metaphors and imagery of orienteering.

Much of the imagery to do with **ambiguity** in this chapter was developed from first principles. It occurred to me that, as we mature, we lose a sense of innocence as we realize just how ambiguous life really is. The biological advantage of ambiguity is more chance for variety; and nature likes variety. Clear-cut decisions seem fewer in number as we age. The imagery in Chapter 8 is designed to aid the understanding that a healthy amount of 'tug' between opposing forces is actually a good thing.

Polarity Management™ shows that we now have the means to maintain useful tensions based on a clear understanding of why we should take the strain. See *Polarity Management™* by Barry Johnson, published 1992, 1996 by HRD Press, Inc., Amherst, Massachusetts, 800-822-2801, www.hrdpress.com

Apparently scientists can, by a sound test, relatively easily differentiate between a typically **male brain** and a typically **female brain**. Life is never so simple as to allow such an easy division because some women have a typically male brain and some men have a typically female brain. No inference on sexual preferences can be made or is intended by this division. Psychologists and scientists are looking principally at patterns of thinking exhibited in the majority of males and females. For more on the hard-wired differences between how male and female brains work, see *Brain Sex* by Anne Moir and David Jessel, published 1989 by the Penguin Group. See also D. Kimura, 'Male Brain, Female Brain: The Hidden Difference', *Psychology Today* (November 1985), pp. 51–8; D. Kimura, 'Sex Differences in the Brain', *Scientific American*, 267 (1992), pp. 81–7; and D. Kimura, 'Sex, Sexual Orientation and Sex Hormones Influence Human Cognitive Function', *Current Opinion in Neurobiology*, 6 (1996), pp. 259–63. Extensive research and review work by Doreen Kimura indicates that attempts to explain differences in the way we think based upon gender or hormones are difficult because of the complexity of possible influences at work.

Chapter 9

The imagery of **graphs and curves** originated from my time as a genetics student in the early 1970s. I didn't enjoy statistical mathematics but I did see sense in the shapes. Several genetic features could not be explained in simple terms. A variety of shapes helped me imagine gradations of a feature based upon the impact of multiple genes. The same imagery helped me when it came to thinking about business issues. Wave forms feature in sales and marketing proposals where up-front investment is needed prior to launch: products are often initially loss making, followed by a break-even point and then growth.

Graph models can be quite useful if you see your experiences as linear. I'm indebted to Graham Rawlinson who first showed me his compound graph of life. Graham is very creative and is currently writing books on invention and innovation. He can be contacted at Graham@dagr.demon.co.uk or www.dagr.demon.co.uk

Chapter 10

Reached the top and still not in control! There is a note in Rick Semlars' *Maverick*, published 1994 by Arrow, Random House, in which Rick explains he once thought collapsing from overwork was what people did. Then the penny dropped and he tried a smarter way. Also see *Moments of Truth* by Jan Carlzon, published 1987 by Ballinger and 1989 by HarperCollins. In the same vein, see James A. Belasco and Ralph C. Sayer, *Flight of the Buffalo*, published 1994 by Warner Books.

Chapter 11

On **creativity**, *Synectics* by W.J.J. Gordon, published 1961 by Harper and Row, is a classic. The word synectics was invented to describe 'the joining together of two different and apparently irrelevant elements'. Synectics is also a globally active company specializing in creative work with organizations.

Thinker Toys is a very good 'how to' book. It was published 1991 by Ten Speed Press, Box 7123, Berkeley, CA 94707.

There are several books on creativity by Edward de Bono and most are accessible. If you only have time to read one, see *Serious Creativity*, published 1992 by HarperCollins.

For inspiration for **analogies and rich pictures**, see any good dictionary or gardening book, any richly illustrated magazine, any tales of epic journeys and Gareth Bryan-Jones, *Orienteering Techniques*, published 1994 by SOA.

For a sense of **humour**, see the full-colour, pocket-sized *Orbiting the Giant Hairball – A Corporate Fool's Guide to Survival* by Gordon Mackenzie, first published 1996 by OpusFoccus, my copy published 1998 by Viking/Penguin.

Chapter 12

The first move to **knowing yourself** is to listen to yourself. Books in this region that might inspire you could come from anywhere. These might include religious, philosophical or humorous sources. I can also recommend Greek mythological tales as a rich source. Here are some more specific recommendations.

First, *The Art of War* by Sun Tzu (500BC); there are other translations but my copy is translated by Samuel B. Griffith, published 1963 by Oxford University Press. *The Prince* by Machiavelli (c.1512) was considered forbidden reading material or at worst demonic because it was one of the first considered works on *realpolitik*. My copy is a translation by George Bull, published 1961, 1973 and subsequently by Penguin. By reading the book with analogies in mind, you can derive present-day lessons quite easily. If you do decide to read Machiavelli's dark little book, you should also read, by way of a suitable antidote, *The Prophet* by Khalil Gibran. This was first published in the early 1900s and is a highly worthwhile pocketbook of philosophy where care and love are important. It is widely available today.

It is not my aim to promote or denigrate any particular religious belief-system. The selection below is merely what I have read; the omission of other sources is not intentional. I have found useful lessons from all of the following. For abstract inspiration, try a book by an older contemporary of Confucius – Lao Tzu, c.500BC – called *Tao Te Ching, or, The Book of The Way.* The copy I have is an English translation by Stephen Mitchell, published 1996 by Kyle Cathie, first published in Great Britain by Macmillan 1989. I also find inspiration by dipping at random into Deng Ming-Dao, *Everyday Tao, Living with Balance and Harmony* published 1996 by Harper San Francisco.

Finally, reading the Book of Proverbs from a modern Bible reminds us of how durable common sense is over thousands of years. See in particular Proverbs 16:32.